*Dedicated to the brave and courageous women and girls of the South who faced unknown threats and atrocities by the invading heathens from the North.*

*But, through it all, they stood steadfast — unbowed and unconquered.*

# SHERMAN'S RASCALS

*A Collection of Essays on the Atrocities of Sherman's March Through the Carolinas*

*Compiled by Frank B. Powell, III*

*Foreword by Karen Stokes*

Wake Forest, NC
www.scuppernongpress.com

*Sherman's Rascals*
*A Collection of Essays on the Atrocities of Sherman's March Through the Carolinas*

Compiled by Frank B. Powell, III
Foreword by Karen Stokes

©2015 The Scuppernong Press

First Printing

The Scuppernong Press
PO Box 1724
Wake Forest, NC 27588
www.scuppernongpress.com

Cover and book design by Frank B. Powell, III

All rights reserved. Printed in the United States of America.

No part of this book may be reproduced or transmitted in any form or by any means, electronic or mechanical, including photocopying, recording, or by any information and storage and retrieval system, without written permission from the editor and/or publisher.

International Standard Book Number ISBN 978-1-942806-04-2

Library of Congress Control Number: 2015915169

# Contents

Introduction .................................................................... iii

Foreword ......................................................................... v

When The Federals Passed Through Our Community ....... 1

One Account of Sherman's Raid ........................................ 9

Sherman's March Through the Carolinas ......................... 13

A North Carolina Child of the Confederacy .................... 21

For My Children ............................................................. 25

Incidents of the Invasion of North Carolina .................... 35

My Personal Experience of War ...................................... 41

Courage Displayed in the Face of Overwhelming Odds ... 47

When the Two-Horse Buggy Came Down the Street ....... 57

Bibliography ................................................................... 69

# ⇛ Introduction ⇚

It must have been fate when I first stumbled upon these essays on the 150th anniversary of the events which they describe. Already politically correct so-called historians were spouting off about Sherman not being such a bad guy — he had been misunderstood by past historians — and other such nonsense.

But, the following short stories prove otherwise. In fact, had the South succeeded in its quest for independence, Sherman would have been tried for war crimes. He had full knowledge of the atrocities his men were committing and could have put a stop to it — but he didn't!

Sherman and his men, I can't call them soldiers, made war on women, children and old men, innocent civilians who were just trying to survive while their fathers, husbands, brothers and sons were on the front lines defending hearth and home. This was unheard of in the annals of civilized countries.

War is never pretty, there is always suffering and destruction, but there was no justification for the actions of Sherman's men.

The ladies who wrote about their experiences wanted future generations to know about their trials and tribulations in the spring of 1865. Their stories have been almost forgotten, but they are printed in these pages for you to read and study, and to pass on to generations yet to come. For if one generation forgets, these stories will be lost for all eternity. Let's not let this happen!

The bravery, courage, devotion and defiance shown over and over again by the women and girls of the South is inspiring. It is a story not told in our politically correct world which seems intent on eradicating our Southern culture and traditions. It is my hope you too will be inspired and share these stories with family and friends.

I would like to thank Karen Stokes for her excellent foreword. She is an accomplished historian and a great writer. Please make sure you read her words before starting the essays.

*Deo Vindice!*

*— Frank B. Powell, III, Editor*

*This chicken is on the steeple of Christ Church in Raleigh, NC, and is a local celebrity in that he has the distinction of being the only chicken not taken by Sherman's army during its occupation of Raleigh. "He is a great old bird," writes Miss Martha Haywood of Raleigh, "and has watched the wedding and burial of many a loyal son and daughter who gave all for the Stars and Bars." He still stands on his perch today.*

# Foreword

In the winter of 1865, the home front in the Carolinas became a war front for thousands of civilians. Most able-bodied men of military age were away from their homes fighting in the Confederate army, and their wives, children, parents, grandparents and family servants faced the onslaught of General William T. Sherman's invading, destructive army without protection. Many of these civilians left behind a record of their encounters with the enemy in the form of letters and diaries written at the time, and in memoirs and other accounts published later.

After completing his "March to the Sea" through Georgia, General Sherman captured the city of Savannah in December 1864. The following month, his forces moved into South Carolina and began to cut a broad swath of destruction across the state, burning farms, plantations, and towns, demolishing railroad lines, destroying or confiscating crops and livestock, and plundering and abusing civilians, reducing them to hopelessness and destitution. Having been the first state to secede from the union, South Carolina was singled out for particularly savage treatment by the Northern army, and in my book *South Carolina Civilians in Sherman's Path*, I chronicle the harrowing experiences of many of her people.

Sherman's army entered North Carolina in early March 1865 and began a northward march to Fayetteville. In his book *Merchant of Terror: General Sherman and Total War* (which I highly recommend), historian John B. Walters noted that, "Immediately upon crossing into North Carolina the conduct of the Federal troops underwent a pronounced change." Several of Sherman's generals remarked on the improvement in conduct of the soldiers, who had been given orders expressing the hope that "every effort will be made to prevent any wanton destruction of property, or any unkind treatment of citizens."

It is true that North Carolina did not see the scale of ruthless destruction, plunder and criminality which had been visited on South Carolina, but as the stories in this book will demonstrate, a number of Sherman's soldiers continued to commit crimes against civilians (and these crimes were continued even after the war ended by occupying Federal troops in North Carolina). Official records of the war also attest to the fact that all of Sherman's troops did not suddenly transform into exemplary soldiers upon crossing the state line into North Carolina.

On April 12, as Sherman's army was marching from Goldsboro to Raleigh, one of his officers, Major General Jacob D. Cox of the 23rd Corps, issued a Circular which stated in part, "Since we left Goldsborough there has been a constant succession of house burning in rear of this command." A week later, on April 19, General O. O. Howard, Sherman's second in command, issued Field Order no. 15, which stated:

*No more animals or subsistence stores will be taken from the inhabitants without the special direction of division or corps commanders. Great disregard has been shown in many instances to the orders heretofore issued on the subject, and many of the poor people of the surrounding country are entirely deprived of their provisions…and animals, which are worthless to us, but are invaluable to them to enable them to raise crops for the subsistence of people…Precautions must be taken… corps and division commanders to provide against the robbing of the people.*

On May 9, 1865, at Greensboro, General H. Judson Kilpatrick reported to General Schofield in Raleigh, "A soldier of my command killed an old man to-day, a citizen, because he would not give up his money." (In South Carolina, it had been a common practice among Sherman's soldiers to hang or threaten to hang civilians, usually old men, in order to force them to reveal where they had hidden their valuables.) Official army correspondence and reports also record that outrages were being committed against North Carolina women by Sherman's army and by occupying forces after the war. In early May 1865, General Davis Tillson reported that two Federal soldiers "stole out of camp on the march to Asheville and committed rape on the person of a young white woman, after nearly killing her uncle and aunt, two very old people, who tried to prevent the outrage."

In South Carolina, a number of black women were victimized in this way by Sherman's soldiers, as were some white women, although this crime, regarded in the Victorian era as hideously shameful and a "fate worse than death," was seldom publicly acknowledged. In *The*

*Illustrated Confederate Reader,* historian Rod Gragg noted, "In their search for hidden treasure, Sherman's troops sometimes coarsely searched Southern women, ripping open dresses and hoisting skirts. Accounts of rape, however, appear to have been voluntarily suppressed. Such assaults were regarded as the worst fate that could befall a lady." Gragg goes on to relate the story of Clara Maclean, "a rural North Carolina homemaker…who openly discussed her experience when the worst nearly occurred." Mrs. Maclean's story, published in the *Southern Historical Society Papers* in 1885, was a first person account of her encounter with a menacing "blue-coat" during the last days of the war.

When Mrs. Maclean saw Yankee soldiers riding up to her house, she armed herself with a dagger, or stiletto. She watched as several of the men looted valuables from her house, and followed one upstairs. This soldier, who claimed to be "looking for arms," demanded that she open a locked trunk, and she complied. She continued:

> The first object that met his eye — well trained in such service — was a tiny morocco purse. "Ha! What's that?"
>
> I took it up and unclasped it tenderly. There lay one poor little silver sixpence, my only remaining bit of specie, which I had kept "for luck." There also nestled a miniature Confederate Flag that had been wont to adorn my toilette as a breast-knot in happier days, and was endeared by a thousand sweet memories.
>
> "This is all the money I have in the world," I said, holding up the sixpence, "but you can have it if you wish."
>
> He threw it aside with an impatient gesture and another oath and walked off. Before I was aware of his intention, he had locked the door. I rose and walked toward it. "Come," I said, "and I will show you the trunks in the other room, as there is nothing here, you see, in the way of arms."
>
> But he had stationed himself in front of the door, his back toward it. For a moment, nay, a long minute — centuries it seemed to me — we stood thus. There he was, a stalwart blonde of perhaps twenty-three or four, over six feet in height; his breath hot with the peach brandy they had unearthed on this raid; his eyes blood-shot, a reckless demon looking out of their grey-green depths, ready for any atrocity. I measured him from cap to boots, then fixed my eyes steadily on his,

not fearful in the least, calm to petrification almost, only as I pressed my left hand against my side I felt there a strange, wild fluttering, as of an imprisoned bird. With the other I slowly and stealthily unloosed the stiletto from its sheath, for it stuck tightly in the silver scabbard, and still gazed at him with unflinching nerves and tense muscles.

Whether he saw and divined the movement, or whether he heard his companions galloping away, I know not; or if indeed any "means" were necessary in this wonderful intervention of a protecting Providence. I only spoke these words very low, and my own voice was strange to me in its vibrating intensity, "What do you mean, sir? Open that door!"

One moment more his eye retained its fiendish brightness, then drooped. He turned, unlocked the door, and went down, I following...

When I went to my room that night it was not to sleep. In the flickering fire-light ... I lived again, over and over a hundred times, the fearful experiences of that brief afternoon. Not until then, in the silence and loneliness of midnight, did I realize the unutterable peril with which I had been threatened. As the ghostly shadows danced over the wall, I seemed to see the athletic frame looming up out of the darkness, the fierce fair face, yet lit up with a baleful glare, staring at me till I was turned to stone. For many weeks and months this fearful vision filled my waking hours as it did my dreams, and not even the distance of twenty years has dimmed a memory so fraught with horror.

In 1866, North Carolina author Cornelia Phillips Spencer published *The Last Ninety Days of the War in North Carolina*, a book recounting many of the crimes committed against civilians by Sherman's army in the state. After describing a number of these incidents, including the plunder of private residences at Fayetteville, Goldsboro and Asheville, the burning of houses, and the hanging of a number of male citizens until they were nearly dead, Spencer explained her reasons for writing the book:

If it be asked why these have been presented, and why I seek to prolong these painful memories, and to keep alive the remembrances that ought rather to slumber and be forgotten with the dead past, let me reply that it is deliberately, and of set purpose, that I sketch these outlines of a great tragedy for our Northern friends to ponder. The South has suffered; that they admit in general terms, and add, "Such is war." I desire to call their attention to the fact that such is NOT war, as their own standards declare; that the career of the grand army in the Great March, brilliant as was its design, masterly as was its execution, and triumphant as was the issue, is yet, in its details, a story for which they have no reason to be proud, and which, if truly told, if there be one spark of generosity, one drop of the milk of human kindness in Northern breasts, should turn their bitterness toward the South into tender pity, their exultation over her into a manly regret and remorse. They do not know — they shall never know unless Southerners themselves shall tell the mournful story — what the sword hath done in her fair fields and her pleasant places.

The stories which follow in this book were written for the same reason.

— Karen Stokes

*Karen Stokes, an archivist with the South Carolina Historical Society in Charleston, SC, is the co-editor of* Faith, Valor, and Devotion: The Civil War Letters of William Porcher DuBose, *published by the University of South Carolina Press in 2010, and* A Confederate Englishman: The Civil War Letters of Henry Wemyss Feilden *(USC Press, March 2013). She is also the author of two non-fiction books published by The History Press,* South Carolina Civilians in Sherman's Path *(June 2012), and* The Immortal 600: Surviving Civil War Charleston and Savannah *(2013). Her historical fiction includes* Belles: A Carolina Love Story *(2012), inspired by the wartime letters of South Carolinians,* The Soldier's Ghost: A Tale of Charleston *(2014), and her newly released* Honor in the Dust, *a novel set in wartime South Carolina.*

# When the Federals Passed Through Our Community

## By Mrs. A. B. Douglas

"The Yankees are coming!" What terror that warning cry brought to the hearts of the Southern people, in the early days of 1865, we can never know. The news of wanton destruction practiced by Sherman and his hordes traveled ahead of them, and those whose homes were in the path of his "triumphant march," knew what lay in store for them.

On the march, his men spread out over an area of from twenty-five to fifty miles-stealing, burning, and otherwise destroying what they could not use or carry off with them. It has been claimed that the soldiers were given orders to burn nothing but cotton gins and houses in which cotton was stored. If they were given this order, they certainly did not obey it.

On reaching Columbia, South Carolina, the Yankees' guns were placed on a hill across the Congaree River, and for three days they practiced getting the range — using the State House (the Capitol) as the target. On the west side of this large building may be seen, today, six iron stars, each marking the spot where a shell struck.

Leaving destruction in his wake, Sherman and his army evacuated the burning city on the morning of February 18, 1865, and went into camp six miles north of Columbia in a locality known as "Lightwood Knot Springs," a famous camp of instruction for Confederate soldiers. During the several days and nights that the army remained in camp, the work of destroying the railroad, then known as the Charlotte and Columbia, was pushed with vigor by a detail from the army.

The work of destruction as carried on by these men was novel, interesting, and spectacular. Equipped with tools made for the purpose, they tore from the roadbed the iron rails, cross-ties, and stringers, that made up the road at that time. They then proceeded to pile the timber along the side of the roadbed, on fills, and in cuts. After these were set on fire, the iron rails (little chub) were laid on top. When the rails had reached a white heat, the fireman, with tongs, hooks, and levers would take them from the fire and twist them into all manner of shapes. This, they thought, rendered the rails useless for all time. Another method used was to twist them around a tree or telegraph pole, leaving them — when cold — resembling snakes wrapped around the trees and poles. Thus the men detailed for that purpose proceeded to completely destroy about sixty miles of track, before leaving the railroad at Blackstock. The railroad shops in Columbia had been burned, and all cars and engines rendered useless. Scattered along the line between Chester, South Carolina, and Charlotte, North Carolina, and points further north, was all the rolling stock that had not been destroyed.

While Sherman's men were so thoroughly rendering the railroad useless, one of the section masters was looking on. An officer remarked to him, "Old man, what are you going to do when we are gone? There'll be no job for you."

The section master replied, "1 will be getting ready to build the road again just as soon as you are out of sight." "We have left you nothing to build with," said the officer.

"There are pine trees in the woods yet, and I will take the twists out of the rails as sure as you are born," was the section master's answer. For this speech the officer was about to take him along as a prisoner, but finally let him go. Little did these men, viewing their handiwork, think that what the section master said would really come to pass before many months.

As the raiders (they scarcely deserve to be called soldiers) moved northward from Columbia, their path lay through Fairfield and Chester counties, in which my father and my mother lived, respectively.

My father's home was about ten miles from Winnsboro, the county seat of Fairfield County, which joins Richland County, where Columbia is situated. About the same distance, or less, from his home were a number of large plantations where lived his relatives or friends. He and his three brothers volunteered for the Confederate service as soon as Lincoln's broken promise forced the firing of the first gun. At home were his father (John G. Brice), too old for service; his mother (Jeannette); and four sisters, one a young widow with a tiny baby girl. Practically all of the servants remained faithful and true to their master and mistress, not only during the war but through the worse days of Reconstruction. One of the most devoted and dependable among them was Ben.

When they heard that the Yankees were coming-stealing and burning as they came — it was Ben who helped "Marse John" and

"Miss Jinny" to hide what valuables they could. But all too soon the dreaded Yankees began to arrive. They swarmed all over the house, rummaging through everything, taking what they wanted and throwing the rest aside, to be trampled under their muddy boots.

The place of chief interest to them was the kitchen, a house consisting of one very large room with a huge fireplace in which hung old fashioned cranes, with three-legged iron ovens or "spiders," in which bread was baked, in the corners of the wide hearth. Two smaller rooms and a large attic served for storage. The kitchen was about fifty feet from the house (to lessen the danger of fire, I was told) but this was no hardship since the cook had several helpers to carry the meals, in covered dishes, to the huge dining room.

The Yankees ordered the cook to prepare food, and while the orders were-perforce-being obeyed, they spread all over the yard and surrounding premises. They raided the smokehouse and loaded all the cured meat into wagons (most of them stolen), caught and killed all the turkeys, geese, chickens and guineas that they could find, some of which they ordered the cook and her helpers to prepare for them to eat. The rest they put into their knapsacks and into bags to carryon to the next camp. They took all the potatoes, turnips, and other vegetables stored in the cellar, and all dried fruits-thus leaving the yard and pantry absolutely bare of food of any kind.

They took all the hay, fodder, and corn from the barns and corn-cribs, and carried it out to where their horses were picketed. They then butchered hogs and cows, took what they could have cooked, then; and what they wanted to take to the next camp, and left the greater part to spoil. No reason is known for their making no attempt to burn the house, unless it was because the amount of stolen food so pleased them that they didn't think of it. It was certainly no kindly gesture because, on a neighboring plantation, the soldiers — after plundering and stealing as they did at my grandfather's and all other homes, within many miles, took pieces of "lightwood" (rich pine wood, usually knots), set them on fire and went into all the bedrooms and put them under the big four-poster beds. As soon as the Yankees left the house, the family and servants managed to put out the fire, although the bedding was badly damaged and some was entirely destroyed. This was the way that Sherman's men treated — in many, many instances — the families who made no resistance whatever.

They took all the best horses and mules from my grandfather's stables and pastures, leaving some broken-down ones of their own, that were of no further use to them. Then this army that found it necessary to starve women and little children, moved on to another plantation to go through the same procedure.

When the Yankees were finally out of the house, my grandmother at once began a search for some food which could be prepared for the family, particularly for the three-year-old granddaughter, and for the servants. The pantry and store-room were empty, not even a cupful of flour or meal could be found. My grandmother told Ben to get the other Negro men and go see what could be found, and that was some corn that the horses had not eaten-all trampled in the dirt; and some that the Yankees had deliberately scattered over the hills, when they found they had more than was needed for the horses.

The Negroes gathered this up and put it into sacks, which they carried on their backs to the nearest gristmill where they had it ground into meal. While the greedy, savage, so called "soldiers" of William Tecumseh Sherman feasted on food stolen from helpless people, a baby cried for something to eat.

While they did not burn the house, they did burn the gin house and cotton press, located about a quarter of a mile from the house, and about two hundred bales of cotton — most of it already baled, and the rest in lint cotton — and a large quantity of cotton seed.

In the county seat of Fairfield County — Winnsboro, a town of about three thousand people, on the railroad between Columbia and Charlotte, which was being completely destroyed-similar outrages were taking place. The people there could see, at night, the reflection on the sky of the flames of the burning Capital and of many country homes nearby.

Rumors were afloat that orders had been given not to burn Winnsboro, but as the "barbarians from the North" (as the people of South Carolina and Georgia had just cause to call them) swooped down on this peaceful, aristocratic little town, the inhabitants soon realized that the rumors were false.

In Winnsboro there lived a gifted woman — Mrs. Catherine Ladd — who conducted a school for girls, where two of my father's sisters were attending at the outbreak of the war. When Sherman's horde swarmed into town and began their looting and burning, a guard was placed at Mrs. Ladd's house because a Yankee officer had seen a Masonic Chart in the house.

As house after house was set on fire and the flames came nearer this house that held the Chart, the officer rode up, dashed into the house, and came out carrying the Chart. He gave orders to some of his men to dig a hole in the garden, place the Chart between mattresses, and bury it.

Mrs. Ladd, realizing that this man was a member of the Masonic Order, asked him to follow her and together they rushed into the Masonic Hall, which was already blazing, and saved the Masonic jewels, but were prevented by smoke and flames, from saving anything else. Mrs. Ladd quickly carried the box of jewels to a place of safety, then returned to her house, which was, by this time, burning. The officer ordered his men to carry out her piano, which they did — but with the loss of one of its legs. Strangely, a neighbor's piano was burned all except one leg, and it matched Mrs. Ladd's piano perfectly. All her other possessions were lost.

Some of the heartless vandals carried the melodeon from the Episcopal Church, where it had been used for many years, and, as one of them played some uncouth tune, the others leaped and danced, like heathen savages, while the Church burned and the terror-stricken women begged for mercy and tried to comfort and protect their little children, screaming with fear. Above the roar of the flames could be heard the taunts and curses of the relentless enemy.

Moving northward, leaving destruction and want behind him, Sherman heard — through his scouts — that General Wheeler ("Fighting Joe") was at Chester, county seat of Chester County, and was rapidly moving south to meet him. Sherman apparently had no desire to encounter Wheeler, because he gave orders for his army to turn east. The first troops were by that time at Blackstock, a small town on the line between Chester and Fairfield counties, and only twelve miles from the town of Chester. Just on the edge of Blackstock they turned right on a road leading east.

About nine miles from Blackstock, on this road, in Chester County, was my mother's childhood home. At the beginning of the war, her sixteen-year-old brother volunteered at once; her father — Robert B. Caldwell — tried to enlist but, because of his age, was not accepted. As soon as there were wounded soldiers, he went to Virginia to nurse them. My grandmother-Mary Lucinda Neely — with her five little children, the oldest (my mother) ten years old, and the youngest only a few weeks old, bravely looked after the home with the help of her good and loyal servants.

Early in 1863, she died, and the care of the little children fell on the shoulders of my mother, then thirteen. The house servants —cook, nurse, house girl, and seamstress had been well trained by my grandmother and carried on the housework; while Rube, the carriage driver, looked after the yard boys and outside work, carrying out my grandfather's directions when he was away.

Soon after the dread news, that Sherman was near, reached them, they saw the long line of blue-clad men coming down a long red clay hill, known as the "Moffatt Hill," because the Moffatt family lived at the top. At the bottom of the hill was a creek, and the men were hidden from sight by the thick woods until they reached the top of the next hill — not far from my grandfather's home. My mother — a frightened little girl — with the other little children; the nurse, holding the baby; and the other terrified Negroes, waited, helpless.

Because Sherman did not know just how near Wheeler's army was, his men were ordered to keep on the march. They were so eager to get out of the way of the Confederates that they had no time to live up to the reputation which they had earned and so richly deserved. They were afraid to fight men!!!

This, and this only, is the reason that my grandmother's beautiful "coin silver" was not carried off to grace the table of some family in the North, but is still treasured by members of the family.

The Yankees took what food they could grab on the march, but the long blue line kept steadily moving east, to join the other troops that had turned east on roads further to the south, taking them by Camden, Cheraw, and other towns, before they turned north into North Carolina.

One of General Wheeler's scouts was J. C. (Jake) Warren, of Sweetwater, Tennessee. He frequently stayed in the Caldwell home while on his trips to get information for General Wheeler, regarding Sherman's movements and plans. Years afterward, when I was a child, he came back to South Carolina to visit again the scenes of his many adventures, and was a guest in our home. When he and my father sat and talked over "the war," I was always an intensely interested listener, and asked many questions. Mr. Warren said that he had an old Yankee overcoat and cap, and with that disguise he went anywhere. He said, with a chuckle, that if he was told to go around Sherman's army, he went through. Only one time was he suspected. A sentry stopped him, as he was taking the horse of one of the generals, but Mr. Warren was quicker, disarmed him and took him along. When asked what he did with the Yankee, all he would say was, "I lost him." For a long time after listening to his experiences, this incident was confused in my mind with the account of David's taking the spear and cruse of water from King Saul's tent.

## BIBLIOGRAPHY

1. Information obtained from my father — W. Watt Brice, Co. F., 12th Regiment, South Carolina Volunteers; from my mother — Carrie Caldwell Brice; from Wheeler's scout — J. C. Warren.

2. Old newspaper clippings from *The Fairfield News and Herald*, Winnsboro, SC; and *The State*, Columbia, SC.

Submitted by Katharine Kinloch.

# One Account of Sherman's Raid

## By Jane Dickinson DeRosset

*Severely wounded in Virginia and forced to resign from service, Colonel Robert H. Cowan of the 18th North Carolina Regiment became president of the Wilmington, Charlotte and Rutherfordton Railroad Company in the spring of 1863, and removed his family to a home about five miles from Laurinburg in Scotland County, and about twenty miles from Cheraw, South Carolina. From here he oversaw railroad operations for the remained of the war. His daughter Jane Dickinson DeRosset was a young girl at that time and recalled the following:*

"I shall never forget when Sherman's army reached [Cheraw, and opposed primarily by General Wade Hampton's cavalry forces, under General Joseph E. Johnston], during the first week of March in 1865.

We sat and listened all day to the booming of the cannon, with aching hearts and fervent prayers that the enemy might be driven back — the utter desolation when we knew that Johnston's Army had passed by and we were left alone to face the dreaded foe!

Late that afternoon I sat on the front steps at my father's feet trying to comfort him and to receive comfort from him, for we were in the deepest distress, our whole country devastated, our dear Southern boys retreating, but contesting every inch of ground, falling by the wayside, gladly giving up their life-blood for the land they loved so well. The brave, noble remnant struggling on, overpowered by numbers, yet full of faith and trust in their leaders, striving to reach Lee and join forces.

Then all would be well.

Besides this, the angel of Death lowered over our house. My youngest sister (now Mrs. Junius Davis) and brother had been ill for weeks with scarlet fever, and our physician had that day given up all hope of saving them. The burden seemed greater than we could bear. Every minute we expected [my sister and brother] to leave us and the Federal troops to be upon us.

Once we heard the tramping of horses [for as the] day broke I looked out the window and from every direction the hated blue uniforms were coming. They seemed to spring out of the ground and in a few seconds our house was full of them.

They were everywhere, upstairs and downstairs, rummaging through closets, trunks, bureaus, wardrobes, anywhere, until every piece of silver, jewelry, clothing and everything else, including food, was gone. We spent the whole day without one mouthful to eat. Our [black] servants came crying and saying they tried to bring us something, but the [Northern] men would snatch it from them.

My mother had a spoon in which she was mixing medicine for her sick children snatched from her, and she was obliged to mix it in her hand and put it into their mouths with her finger. They pulled the rings from her fingers as she was holding in her lap, and kicked the cradle in which the other one was lying, with the remark, "That one is dead already."

One of the soldiers engaged in this indignity had meanwhile stood with his loaded musket beside the chair in which my mother sat. They were yelling, cursing, drinking, pitching trunks and boxes from the attic down two flights of stairs to the first floor, breaking them open and putting all that could be carried in that way about their persons, piling up the rest and making bonfires of them.

We had trunks of valuables belonging to General [William H.C.] Whiting], which he had sent us for safe-keeping when the city of Wilmington had fallen into the hands of the foe; also had all that Bishop Watson, who was at that time rector of Saint James Church in Wilmington, had saved when the town of New Berne, NC, fell.

One of them rushed into the room where we were all gathered together, dressed in the Confederate uniform of my uncle, Captain John Cowan, and going up to my grandmother, slapped her face with Confederate money which he had found somewhere about the house, grabbed at her watch guard, which she thought she had hidden, and pulled it with the watch from her neck. I was thankful my father was then out of the room, but he soon came in with a Federal soldier, who had promised him to protect us; though he really had no authority in doing so (this man we found afterwards was a North Carolinian and a deserter from the Confederate army).

There were five watches taken from us at that time. Another [soldier] came up to me, a girl of sixteen, and told me to give him a ring, which I did not have. My younger sister … said that if he would

leave me alone she would give him one, and as he took it, he threw his arms around her saying he was a Philadelphia boy and had just come out of the penitentiary, which we could well believe.

My father sprang forward....[and] I thought we would all be killed, but Providence watched over us. I saw a [soldier] put a pistol to my father's head and another knock it aside just as it went off. We had begged father the night before to leave us and go into the woods with our brother and uncle, for we were afraid he would be killed, but he would not go.

[My father] had been in the [Secession] Convention of 1861, which had carried the State out of the Union, and the soldiers had found one of his speeches and had fastened it up on the wall where it could be read by all, and when our uncle, Dr. McRee, asked for a guard for our house and told the officers how outrageously their men were behaving, they answered that they did not care what they did at our house, for they had heard of Colonel Cowan all through South Carolina.

*As night came, the [deserter] guard told my father he must take his family out of that house....[and that] when the rest of the army came up that night he would not answer for the consequences, so after dark we stole quietly through [the enemy] camp to an old temperance hall about a quarter mile away. It had been roughly fixed up as a dwelling for Dr. McRee's family, and in that old shanty we remained for a week (while the Union Army was passing), with nothing to eat, nothing to wear, nothing to look forward to but death.*

Sometimes our servants would steal a chicken or turkey from the soldiers and bring it to us, and we would hold in with our hands over the fire until it was cooked enough for us to eat, and that would be all we would have for a day or two.

At last one afternoon the Negro regiments were coming up and they surrounded the old hall yelling that we had gold hid and they were going to have it. I certainly thought then, as we looked out on that sea of black faces, that our time had come, and that death or worse was near.

We barred the doors and windows, and my father got out and walked through those regiments until he found a general, who after hearing him, ordered the Negroes away, and with his staff spent the night in the lower part of the old hall. [They enjoyed] a good supper, we upstairs had not tasted food all day….[and the Northern] general sent a few pieces of dry baker's bread….

The next day the last of Sherman's army left us, and we started back to our home, which the troops had tried to burn down, but our servants had saved for us. We had nothing but the clothes we had on and a few articles of clothing for the children, and we came to an empty house.

The heavy furniture which could not be carried off was there, and Bibles, Prayer-books and pictures, torn, broken and covered with mustard and molasses.

We had no food but the corn their horses had dropped while eating, which we picked up, washed and ground, and a few potato slips, nothing else. When we found a room that was not full of feathers from the beds that had been torn open [looking for valuables], we threw ourselves down and rested, thanking God that we were alive and had a roof over our heads.

My father told his servants to try to get to Wilmington, where they were known, and could make a living, for he did not know he would get meat and bread for his own family and could not help them, though he would do what he could for those who remained with us."

# Sherman's March Through North Carolina

## *By Mrs. Andrew J. Howell*

When General William T. Sherman entered North Carolina in March 1865, it was not his first visit to the state. Twenty years previous to this time, while serving as an army officer in the South, he had been detailed as a member of a general court-martial, which was sitting at Wilmington. On that occasion he was a welcome guest in the city, and he had great pleasure in meeting many of his former companions in arms.

In 1865 how different the situation! Now he comes, not as a friend, but as an enemy, bent on doing all possible harm to the Southern people.

Just before entering the State he wrote to his lieutenant general: "The army is in splendid health, condition and spirit, although we have had foul weather and roads that would have stopped travel to almost any other body of men I ever heard of. Our march was substantially what I designed. I could leave here tomorrow, but want to clean my columns of the vast crowd of refugees and Negroes that encumber me."

One wonders how this last desire was to be accomplished, and what became of the Negroes, particularly as the records tell us that everywhere Sherman's army went in North Carolina, the soldiers would tell the slaves they were free, and offer to take them along.

Sherman's aim, as he and U. S. General Grant had planned it, was to separate the Carolinas from Georgia on the south and Virginia on the north, and to make Goldsboro in North Carolina his objective and center of operations. In the fall of Fort Fisher in January 1865, and the subsequent fall of Wilmington, the entering wedge had been driven, and the stage set for the entrance of the chief actor.

U. S. General Terry was in command of the southeastern district, with headquarters at Wilmington, U. S. General Schofield was coming from the north-eastern part of the State, trying to re-open the railroads, and U. S. General Stoneman was on the march from the west. From the south, General Sherman, with his powerful army, was marching at a steady rate of about eight miles a day.

To meet this formidable combination, General Lee, recently made commander-in-chief of the Confederate forces, had appointed General Joseph E. Johnston to command the troops in North Carolina. With all the men whom Johnston could assemble, including those under the command of Bragg, Hardee, Hampton, Hood and others, his force numbered only about twenty-five thousand, a much smaller army than that of his enemy.

General Sherman's route through North Carolina was problematical. It was thought that he would march either on Charlotte or on Fayetteville, and at both places preparations were made to receive him. On the 7th of March he entered North Carolina near Laurel Hill. The main body moved towards the northeast, while the cavalry under Kilpatrick marched temporarily towards the west as a feint to make General Johnston believe that the enemy intended to go towards Charlotte.

The roads were now so heavy by reason of the excessive rains that Sherman was forced to move slowly. In some places towards Fayetteville the roads were overflowed and long stretches were "corduroy," that is, made of fence rails, logs, and tree limbs. His slow progress gave Sherman and his men plenty of time to continue their work of destruction. Perhaps not all of the wanton damage wrought should be credited to his regular army; there were many vicious hangers-on, known as "bummers," who stopped at nothing, but they cannot shoulder all the blame by any means. At one plantation after another, the story of woe was the same: homes were ransacked, provisions eaten or wantonly destroyed, furniture confiscated or torn or broken up.

One very old lady remembers the day when Sherman's army reached her plantation home. She relates that they had prepared as far as they could to resist him. The food supplies had been buried in various places, the flat silver had been sewed under the hoop skirts of herself and her mother. About three o'clock in the afternoon the enemy came shooting and yelling, and poured into the yard, a wild, disorderly crew.

With terror in her heart, the mother courteously invited them to dinner. They jeered at the invitation, crowded into the house, turned everything upside down, took what they fancied and destroyed all that they could not carry away.

As the night came on they announced that they needed a light to help them on their way, so they fired the house, and stood guard until it was too far gone to be extinguished. The dear old lady who told this story says that at last she was so full of fury that she ran into the burning house and began frantically to play *Dixie* on her beloved piano. She was pulled out just as the walls collapsed.

Many writers have testified that it was part of the fun of the troops and the bummers to pour molasses on the treasured covers of the plantation beds, to pour out on the ground all liquids and solids which they could not use, and — revolting as it sounds — there were a few low enough to spit into any food in the kitchens which they did not wish for themselves.

Sometimes the bummers met with justice in an unexpected way. One day four of them, swaggering along the road, met three other blue-clad men to whom they gleefully recounted the number of women they had frightened, and the loot they had stolen. Imagine their consternation when their three chance acquaintances sternly ordered them to surrender. They drew their pistols, but not soon enough; and four of Sherman's bummers received quick justice. The blue-clad three were the noted Confederate scout, Shadbourne and two associates, in "borrowed" raiment.

Sherman's army reached Fayetteville on the morning of March 11, after enacting many times, scenes like those narrated above. For several days before that, skirmishes with Kilpatrick and other Union commanders had occurred in various places, but the main body of the Confederate force had left Fayetteville for more strategic points before Sherman came. In Fayetteville his men continued the tactics they had employed in every town they visited.

At one home entered by them, a Negro servant rushed in, exclaiming, "Oh, Miss Susan, they'se done took the dinner Mammy's cooking, and Daddy's Sunday breeches —" then seeing a Yankee officer standing by, he added hastily, "but Daddy don't care!"

The joy and pride of Fayetteville was the Arsenal, once the United States Arsenal, but which had been taken over by the Confederacy when the war began. It was the handsomest collection of buildings in that town of many fine homes. The citadel was a large, oblong three-story building, with an observatory at each end of the roof. There were also three residences for the officials in charge. The grounds were carefully laid out.

Of course such handsome buildings could not escape Sherman's eye. Indeed, it was understood that one of his aims in going through Fayetteville was to burn the Arsenal, which was promptly and thoroughly accomplished, to the horror and despair of the citizens. All the factories, many warehouses, banks, dwellings, stores, the newspaper office, any and every thing that would burn, was fired, and night was as bright as day. The destruction was wrought by the 1st regiment Michigan engineers, under the supervision of Colonel O. M. Poe, chief engineer of the military division.

All of this was accomplished in about three days, incredible as it may seem. Then Sherman left the stricken town. He was moving slowly; he was in no particular hurry. He was receiving supplies from Wilmington, and he and his men were sending a quantity of loot to Wilmington, to be shipped from there to their homes up North. He was also waiting for Schofield to join him. Sherman had ably planned this campaign, and he had really wonderful success in carrying it out. He had fixed upon the vicinity of Goldsboro as the place for a junction with Schofield, and had set March 22 as the time.

There were little skirmishes here and there, such as the one on the 16th of the month when a small detachment of Confederates under

General Hardee was attacked by two corps of Sherman's veterans and Kilpatrick's cavalry at Averasboro on the Cape Fear River. The Confederates were finally forced to retire, but with a loss to the enemy out of all proportion to their respective numbers.

General Johnston, knowing that Sherman was awaiting Schofield's reinforcements before starting the important battle which he had planned, decided to force the issue. By a hard march, he brought his troops into position near the little town of Bentonville on the 19th of March. Fighting began early in the morning. Time after time Sherman attacked, only to be repelled, even with Union reinforcements coming up during the day. When night came the Federals had been forced into an impenetrable thicket, such as can be seen in parts of eastern Carolina today. There they were safe and could rest during the night.

The next morning fighting recommenced, and continued through the day with varying results. On the night of the 20th the enemy abandoned their works. The next day they moved towards Goldsboro, General Johnston going towards Raleigh.

The magnitude and importance of the battle of Bentonville can only be understood if we remember that the Confederate force on the first day was about sixteen thousand infantry and artillery, while there were about thirty-five thousand of the enemy force, and twice that many during the next day's fighting. The Confederate loss for both days was 223 killed, 1,467 wounded. From the appearance of the field, it was estimated the total loss to the enemy must have been more than four thousand.

On the battlefield of Bentonville was fought the last important battle of the war. Here Sherman's destructive march from further South was halted, and who can say how many other towns were saved by the results of this battle. This was the greatest battle waged in North Carolina.

There is little question but that Sherman was exactly in the position which he had planned two months before. His important generals had reached him, and he had arrived at the destination which was his aim for this time. On the 22nd of March he published a congratulatory address to his troops, in which he said:

"After a march of the most extraordinary character, nearly five hundred miles over swamps and rivers deemed impassable to others, at the most inclement season of the year, and drawing our chief supplies from a poor and wasted country, we reach our destination in good health and condition."

Sherman's campaign in North Carolina practically terminated at Goldsboro, and, as soon as he could dispose his army in camp there, he hastened to City Point, Virginia, for an interview with General Grant. President Lincoln was also present. At this time the plan which they seem to have agreed on was that Sherman should attempt to crush Johnston, while Grant should try to crush Lee. A few days later Sherman returned to his army in North Carolina. About this time he issued a report in which he says:

"I cannot with any degree of precision recapitulate the vast amount of injury done the enemy. In general terms we have traversed the country with an average breadth of forty miles, consuming all the forage, horses, cattle, hogs, sheep, poultry, cured meats, cornmeal, etc. The public enemy will be compelled to send provisions from other quarters to feed the inhabitants."

The next plan of Sherman seems to have been to move rapidly northward, feint on Raleigh and strike straight for Burksville, thereby interposing his army between Johnston and Lee. After the battle of Petersburg new plans were made, all of which came to naught when, on April 11, news came to Sherman at Smithfield that Lee had surrendered. On the 14th a flag of truce was received from Johnston, and a meeting was arranged between the two commanders, to take place at Durham Station on the railway between Raleigh and Hillsboro, at 12 o'clock on the 17th.

As General Sherman was leaving to meet Johnston a telegram announcing the assassination of President Lincoln was handed him. When the two generals were finally alone in a farm house near Durham Station, Sherman silently handed the dispatch to Johnston. Sherman writes later that "Johnston denounced the act as a disgrace to the age, and hoped I did not charge it to the Confederate government."

Sherman adds that he had not given the news to his soldiers, then in Raleigh, for fear that they would be so maddened that the fate of Raleigh "would be worse than that of Columbia."

It must be conceded that General Sherman tried to make the terms of surrender reasonable. Perhaps during his recent conference with Lincoln at City Point, he had received instructions from the president to that end. The agreement which Sherman and Johnston agreed upon guaranteed to the people of the subjugated states "their political rights and franchises, as well as their rights of personal property, as defined by the constitution of the United States and of the States respectively."

This humane plan, however, did not take at Washington, and the whole world knows the horrors of Reconstruction which followed.

As soon as the terms of the agreement which had been signed by the two generals reached Washington, Secretary Stanton started a great outbreak of adverse public sentiment, charging that Sherman had been bribed to make easy terms for the South. Many Northern papers denounced him. General Halleck ordered Generals Meade, Sheridan and Wright to advance into his department and pay no regard to any orders from him. Stanton dispatched orders to Sherman's own generals not to obey him, and Sherman was compelled to write Johnston that their agreement must be cancelled.

On May 10th Sherman, with his army, set out for Alexandria, taking nine days to make the trip. What a contrast between his victorious entry into the State and his exit from it, a disappointed man, in disfavor and disgrace with the Union which he had served so zealously!

### Source Material

*Southern History of the War*, Pollard.
*War Days in Fayetteville, NC*, Compiled by the J. E. B. Stuart Chapter, UDC.
*History of North Carolina*, Moore.
*History of the United States of America*, Ridpath.
*Sherman and his Campaigns*, Bowman.
North Carolina UDC Prize Essays.
Old Magazines.
My Scrapbook.

# A North Carolina Child of the Confederacy

## By Mrs. R. C. Pridgen

(NOTE: This story has been told among us until it has become a legend; it has been told of several mothers, grandmothers, aunts, and great aunts; it has been told by many other mothers, grandmothers, aunts and great-aunts; but here it is as it was told me by my own Aunt Susan.)

I was just a child of fourteen years, when the Yankees came through in the spring of '65, although I thought I was quite a young lady, as I had recently been allowed to let down the hem of my homespun dress and to wear my hair up like my mother's. I remember that we had gotten word the day before that Sherman's "rascals" were coming, and we were cooking up a good many rations for them. You see, we realized how much we were at their mercy, so my mother and I, and even my small brother, kept ourselves and what Negroes we had left busy preparing food which we hoped would make them act more kindly toward us. I remember asking my mother how we could get along if the Yankees took all our food, clothes and Negroes.

She said: "Hush, hush, Susan; I don't know, but the 'Lord will provide.'"

My little brother said, "How's the Lord gonna provide if there ain't nothin' left to provide with?" But my mother was, perhaps, too busy to hear him, for she did not reply.

How I hated the Yankees, even as I stirred up a griddle-cake which must go to help feed them. How I prayed that they would not find the things we had hidden, and wondered if they would; for we had hurriedly disposed of our necessary supplies in a number of ways: for instance, we had buried our lard stands under the posts of the grape arbor; our meal bags and sorghum kegs were under the barn floor; our bacon was in the kitchen loft, which could be reached only by a small scuttle hole, and which had no windows; some of our silver was buried, while the flat pieces were wrapped with cloth and sewed to the hoops of my skirts and my mother's. I wore all the clothes I could get on, with my so-called Sunday frock on top.

It was about three o'clock, by sun, I guessed, and my mother and I were sitting on the front porch waiting — for what, we did not know. First we heard shouting and shooting, then we saw a crowd of blue uniforms and horses of different colors coming down the lane. Soon they came up to the big gate where my little brother, who was only eight years old, was watching. Then they poured into the yard. My brother was running crying to my mother.

He cried, "Mother, a Yankee sweared at me. He called me 'a dam' little Reb, cause I wouldn't open the gate quick 'nough.' "

My mother told him, "Ssh! You mustn't be a crybaby, you must be a man. And tell him that it's no disgrace to be a little Rebel."

Then my mother went to the porch steps and addressed the one who seemed to be the leader. I can see her yet, standing there tall, dignified, and grave, showing none of the panic she must have felt. What she said was:

"Will not you and your men take dinner, which we have prepared, with us?"

"O, we may take dinner after there's nothing else left on the place to take," was his answer. War does funny things to men. That Yankee may have been a good man at home; he didn't look so wicked, in the face. It was the dreadful war that made him so hard he could give such orders to the rest of them — orders to burn the mill, to sack the place, to plunder the house, to carry off horses, cows, pigs, anything and everything movable, and destroy the rest — and that they could so liberally carry out his orders, wrecking the home of a defenseless woman and her children. I remember that one of them even went into the kitchen and threw a pail of water on the kitchen fire. The glow of the hearth fire sputtered and died.

We wandered uneasily from place to place, those several hours, not knowing what might happen, for, by sun-down, the Yankees had not eaten the dinner we had prepared, had not left, and were still enjoying themselves, apparently. My mother had not begged nor pleaded for mercy; rather, she had acted as if she were a hostess whose guests were behaving badly, as she had watched, with inward torture, but with outward composure, her most cherished possessions being broken up or carried off. I had sat on the front porch and had

seen Yankees go into our home and come out loaded with our things, among them, my darling pink parasol. When I saw this walk off, my eyes started to fill with tears. My mother noticed this and said sharply, "Susan, what is the matter?"

"Oh"? I told her, "I just sat on a fork." She did not smile. She could not. Nor could I.

About sun-down, the Yankee captain had decided to go on to the next place, to camp there for the night. ' One of the soldiers (I think he had found some whiskey or wine and had drunk it) told us, "Ho, we're leaving now, and I guess you're glad. We need a torch to show us the way to the next place. Come on, let's fire the house!" So they did.

My frantic mother and I, with two of the negroes tried to save a few of what belongings were left to us, while there was still time. The fire, started at the kitchen, had burned its way to the bacon which was still in the kitchen loft. By now, the rest of the house was afire, and we could do nothing more but watch.

I think it was the smell of the frying bacon in the air, mingled with the wood smoke, which made me so mad; for I was both angry and, I think, a little insane. I wanted to 'show those Yankees, to show them that we were not conquered — I wanted to do anything, anything, to prove to them that although we were ruined, our spirit was still unbroken.

I remembered my piano. O, I hoped, I prayed that it should not be afire. No! I could see through the smoke and the parlor window, that the fire had not yet reached it, but I knew that it was doomed. I scrambled through the window, into the smoke-filled room, and groped my way to the piano.

Well, if it must go, the last thing that should ever be played on it would be *Dixie*. I could hear my mother calling faintly; the smoke was almost stifling, as well as blinding; but I found the right keys and began to play. It seemed to me that somebody other than myself was playing the tune which I knew and loved so well. And above the roar of the flames, above the crash of falling timbers, above the shouts of the Yankees, rose the strains of *Dixie*.

It seemed that somebody, who, I knew, must be myself, was singing:

"Then I'll shout hurrah for Dixie! Hurrah! Hurrah!
In Dixie Land I'll take my stand,
To live or die for Dixie.
Away, away, away down South in Dixie,
Away, away, away down South in Dixie."

\* \* \* \*

I must have fainted, for the next thing I knew, my mother was bending over me. I was out of doors, under the cedars, and it was dusk. I looked toward the place where the house had been, and when I saw the heaps of ashes, the still glowing coals, the warped, twisted, blackened timbers, and the big chimney, standing like a tombstone over the grave of our home, I realized the helplessness, the futility, the hopelessness of defeat: and for the first time during that day which I shall never forget, I buried my head in my mother's skirts and wept.

# For My Children

## By Harriet Cobb Lane

A story giving some of the experiences of the War of 1861-1865 and of the times when Sherman fought the last battle of the War at Bentonville, North Carolina, and of the privations of those who lived along the line of its march in Wayne County, North Carolina.

I am a daughter of Mr. William D. Cobb and wife, Ann Collier. My father lived on his plantation nine miles from Goldsboro, Wayne County, on the south side of the Neuse River. He was a stock farmer and did not raise cotton until the war began in 1861. All Southern farmers then raised cotton to help clothe the Confederate soldiers. We did not approve of secession, but wanted to fight for States' Rights under the flag which our fathers had fought for.

I was born and reared on the plantation. Before the war, the planters employed governesses for their children, while young. Then they were sent to preparatory schools before entering college. My sister and I were sent to the Misses Nash and Kellock's Preparatory School in Hillsborough, Orange County, in 1860, and we were there when North Carolina seceded from the Union, and we helped with some of the other school girls, to raise the first Confederate Flag over the Court House. North Carolina seceded May 20th, 1861.

My father gave four sons to the Confederate service. They were among the first to volunteer when Governor Ellis called for volunteers to defend the State. My brothers, Colonel John F. Cobb; Captain Bryan W. Cobb, and Dr. Willam H. N. Cobb, all volunteered as privates, but were made officers in the 2nd Regiment of North Carolina State Troops. My brother, Dr. William H. N. Cobb graduated in Philadelphia, Pennsylvania, just in time to get home and volunteer. At first he was in the 2nd Regiment, but was later transferred to the 4th Regiment as Assistant Surgeon. My fourth brother, Rev. Needham F. Cobb was chaplain of the 4th Regiment; all were first sent to Fort Steel for a few days, then to Virginia, and fought under Lee. My brother Needham's health failed the latter part of the war, and he moved with his family to Raleigh.

After the death of Colonel Charles Yen, (First colonel of the 2nd Regiment), my brother Jon was promoted for bravery on the battlefield, from Captain of Company H to Colonel, and brother Bryan W. Cobb was then made Captain. My brother Dr. W. H. N. Cobb and Capt. Bryan W. Cobb fought through the war and surrendered with Lee at Appomattox. My brother, Col. John Cobb lost a leg in the Battle of Winchester, Virginia, September 19th, 1864, was taken prisoner and confened in Fort McHenry until Lee surrendered.

New Bern fell into the hands of the Yankees, March 21, 1862. My father soon moved his family to a farm four miles from Bentonville (where the last battle of the war was fought 1865). Just after he moved, General Burnside came from New Bern on a march for Goldsboro, passing our place, but our forces had burned the bridge at Spring Bank on New River, six miles from Goldsboro; after being repulsed by our troops, with his army, returned to New Bern.

After a short time my father moved back to his home, and left his daughter, Mrs. Nathan B. Whitfield living there. My father and her husband were members of the Home Guard. After the Battle of Bentonville, Sherman marched to Goldsboro, passing, and resting one night on my father's plantation. The day before Sherman reached our home, my father called his slaves together and said to them, "In a few days you will be free; Sherman will be here and destroy everything; the crop is already planted; he cannot destroy that. We have lived together in peace, as you know; the land, seed, and fertilizer are mine; if you stay and work the crop, you can gather it in two portions; you then select a man and I will select one and these men shall say which portion I am to have." Our Negroes remained on the place and finished the crop.

Sherman had given orders to his troops when he reached Fayetteville to destroy all property, private and public, which would be of any use to the enemy; that he was going to wind up the war. The order is recorded in the Congressional Records of the United States in Washington, D.C. His army carried out his instructions along his line of march. They destroyed our household furniture, leaving the bed on which my sick mother lay, and a large dining table and a few chairs, which were once the property of a Colonial Governor of North Carolina (Governor Tryon) whose furniture was confiscated and sold at auction in New Bern, after the Revolutionary War, and the dining

room suite was bought by my grandfather, John Cobb, of Kinston, North Carolina. This table and chairs were left for Sherman and his officers to use while they rested on our plantation. His army destroyed literally every useful thing, filling all the wells on the place with dead hogs, shooting the cows and all other living things, leaving what they did not want lying on the ground. They rolled all the barrels filled with the year's supply of molasses, into the front hall, burst in the heads, and let the molasses run on the floor, after which they brought quantities of rice, oats, peas, meal, etc. and poured all of this on the molasses; then went up stairs, cut the feather beds and shook the feathers down on it, and then ran horses over it, through the house. They broke out all the window panes, broke doors and window blinds, cut up the carpets and made saddle blankets for their horses. They killed every living thing on the place, except the rats and dogs and carried off all the remaining year's supply of food stuff. My parents and the Negroes lived a few days on the dead fowls. The Yankees moved my mother's maid with her family, into the room adjoining my mother's bed-room thinking they would be humiliated living in the house with their former slaves. These Negroes proved a blessing; they cooked for the Yankees and thus got food for my parents, as long as the army was passing. Of course the dead fowls soon got beyond being useful for food. So after the main army passed, the stragglers who followed put a rope around my father's neck and were going to hang him, but did not, as the Negro men interfered and drove them off. My sister, with her two children, who were then living on the farm near Bentonville, was left alone with her slaves, while her husband was with the Home Guards. No one ever expected Sherman to reach North Carolina by way of Bentonville, but were looking for the Yankees to come from New Bern, Bentonville being the last battle of the war, Sherman made a triumphant march to Orange County, and the last remnant of General Johnson's army of Confederate Soldiers surrendered to him in April 1865. Our Government had a gunboat stationed at Kinston, and trees all along the banks of the Neuse River below the town of New Bern, had been cut and thrown in the river, thus keeping the river free from Yankee boats which might come if New Bern fell. That is why Burnside came by land instead of by boats. Also General Schofield and his army rested on our place while on their way to Goldsboro.

In 1864 my sister and I were day scholars at St. Mary's, Raleigh, but after Richmond fell we quit school and went in the hospitals as nurses. All the wounded from Richmond and Petersburg were brought to Raleigh, and later from Bentonville. Every available place was filled with wounded soldiers: school buildings, fair grounds and private houses. The ladies of Louisburg had sent a car load of cooked provisions to my brother Rev. N. B. Cobb, to be distributed to the retreating army of General Johnson. My parents also had sent a quantity of cooked food before Sherman came to our home, to be given to the wounded men in Raleigh. My brother called some of the Raleigh ladies to help distribute the food. Negro servants were stationed on the side walks along Fayetteville Street, who filled baskets for the ladies who stood on each side of the retreating army. Pore, ragged (barefooted many of them), worn and weary Boys in Gray. The City officials went down to meet Sherman the day before and surrendered the City and asked protection for the people and property. Wheeler's Calvary of the Confederate Army passed through the City at night, next morning, Sherman came marching triumphant up Fayetteville Street, at the head of his army. Several of Wheeler's men had turned back, to fire the depot in which was stored all the remaining ammunition of the Confederacy, and food supplies were piled around the depot. One of the men rode down the street and fired on Sherman, turning down another street, and through several other streets before he was captured near St. Mary's school. Sherman wanted to hang him in Capitol Square but the city officials prevailed on him not to do so. He was killed near St. Mary's. When the bomb shells in the burning depot began to burst, the citizens thought Sherman was waging war on the City. One twelve-year-old white girl was killed by the bursting bombs. Guards were placed at every man's door to prevent angry soldiers from entering private homes.

As soon as a woman was permitted to ride the train, I went with my uncle, Col. George Collier and his wife, back to my old home, and to my distressed parents. After reaching Goldsboro my uncle had to take the oath of allegiance to the U.S. Government before we were furnished a ragged topped ambulance and two old blind cast-off army horses and a Negro driver. We had to cross Neuse River on a pontoon bridge, the real bridge having been burned by our soldiers on their retreat. This bridge was made of planks placed cross-wise on two lines of small boats (or canoes). A regiment of Negro soldiers was stationed there, with white officers. The Colonel placed a line of soldiers on each side of the bridge, and with two more leading the horses, we got in and drove across the bounding bridge in a pouring rain. He had told us to get out before starting across, as the blind horse might turn off and plunge in the river. When we reached home, I found my mother still sick in bed, with her faithful servants waiting on her. My parents and the Negroes were then drawing rations from the Commissary in Goldsboro, the Negroes walking nine miles bringing their portions, and my parents' also, in bags on their backs.

One the plantation was a large Mulberry orchard, planted for the hogs. These berries were ripe when I came home. There was a negro regiment stationed near the house and the white Colonel told my little brother if he would gather and deliver the berries to his soldiers, they would pay him $2 per gallon. The Yankees had destroyed all the vessels on the place and we picked up tin cans (some large and some small) on the camp ground, which Sherman's army had left, and he and the Negroes gathered and delivered many gallons of berries and came back with empty cans and pockets full of greenback money and feeling happy over the prospect of buying better food from somewhere.

My brothers came home with only the clothes on their backs. We borrowed beds, etc. from neighbors who did not live along the line of march, and when my brothers and father changed their underclothes, they went to bed and the Negro women took their clothes to the branch one-fourth mile from the house, where we were all forced to get drinking water, bringing it that distance in cans.

After the Battle of Bentonville my sister was left without food or protection. An officer in blue advised her to take her two children and the two Negro women with her, and leave, as he could not protect her, but not get separated from the two Negroes. She left with them, walking four miles in the woods, just far enough from the marching Yankee army not to be lost of discovered by them; she reached a neighbor, widow Cogdel, whose son, a Confederate soldier had been wounded, and was lying delirious with fever. The Yankees had not been there, and Mrs. Cogdel was having dinner cooked for sister and the children when a squad of Yankees, on horses, rode up, taking her horses, and firing the house in several places. My sister, Mrs. Cogdel, her daughter and the servants carried her son out on a bed, to a field near the house, and there saw the house burn down. Just after sunset, an officer in blue rode up and asked what they were doing there. My sister replied, "To starve and die." After a few minutes he said, "My God, I have a wife and little ones at home," and dashing off soon returned with an ambulance and took them six miles further to a Mr. McCullen's where the Yankees had been, but had not burned the house. They they spent the night. The next morning Mr. McCullen found a cart wheel, and a buggy wheel and an axle which the Yankees failed to cut or burn with other things, and with a few pieces of plank, fixed a conveyance for them to ride in. She then went ten miles to her mother-in-law, Mrs. Sarah Whitfield.

The Yankees had not been there, but while she was giving her experiences quite a lot of them came. She did not live on the line of march, but these men were stragglers from Sherman's Army which had passed on their way to Goldsboro the day before. The old grandmother, 84 years old, lived with her daughter and granddaughter whose sons were in Lee's Army. The deaf old woman had fallen a month before and was in bed with a broken hip. The Yankees ordered her to get up, which she could not do, then one took her by the feet and one took her shoulders, and tossed her across the room, going out, locking the door, bidding none to go out or to come in. It was cool spring weather and a fire was burning; as night came the fire gave light as long as it lasted. The lamps and candles had been taken out before the Yankees came, to be trimmed and washed. As the fire grew low, the old lady begged not to let the light go out. There was a very large box of paper patterns, used to cut the darkies' clothes, in the closet, which my sisters' sister and mother-in-law cut in strips, and one by one was held burning by the old lady's bed. The paper lasted till daybreak. The Yankees destroyed almost everything except what was in their room and a small quantity of provisions. My sister and the two Negroes stayed a few days and then went to my parents. They were riding army horses, bareback, the makeshift vehicle having been destroyed by the last group of stragglers. Theses were horses, which Sherman had deserted when he replenished his army with the horses of the planters along the line.

When she reached home she found devastation and sickness everywhere and the whole air was reeking with dead animals. My father died the following October 20th, 1865 after the crop was gathered. My mother sold a farm in Tennessee, which enabled us to live more comfortably.

Before the Negro regiment stationed on our place was disbanded one of the officers found stored in a barn on the river about four miles from the house, a small quantity of corn which the Yankees had not taken away. He had the corn (a cart load of it) brought up to the house and stored in a bath room at the end of the back hall, upstairs. He had no waterworks or big bath tubs, but did have the nice shower bath closets. The back stairs ran up in this hall, and the windows being broken there was no way to keep the hungry starving rats out, and at night they went up the stairs by hundreds. We would arm ourselves with sticks and beat among them, some nights getting about a peck, and a hand full of tails, and some nights after, we would get the bobtailed rats. The corn proved quite a help in the way of food. We would boil it in lye made from oak ashes, until the husk would come off, then soak it in clear water until all the lye was out of it; then we would cook it until soft and fry it in some of the fat white meat we drew from the Government. This varied our diet of hard tack, fat meat, brown sugar and bad coffee.

We did not drink coffee during the war. My father had an order for coffee and sewing thread, on our blockage steamer whenever she went from Wilmington. The coffee was sent to the boys in the army, and the thread was used on the sewing machine to make their clothes. Our coffee was made of dried sweet potatoes, rye, wheat and barley, all parched brown and ground together, putting some of it in a little bag, we would drop it in the coffee pot of hot water and let it boil ten minutes.

We made all sorts of things during the war. Drugs were hard to get for the hospitals and all kinds of herbs, barks and roots were dried and sent to the hospitals. Large beds of lettuce were planted and let grow a tall stalk, and early in the morning some one would go out with a needle and slit the stalks in several places; the milk would run out and harden on the stalk, and at sunset some one would go with a little knife and piece of paper and collect the hardened drops. This was used as opium; also rose leaves were dried and sent with drugs.

My mother died December 1867. After her death my brother Col. John F. Cobb and his family lived at the old home until he was elected County Court Clerk and moved with his family to Goldsboro and several years later went to Florida. After my mother's death, her land was divided among her children and most of it rented out. Later, after my brother moved to Goldsboro, none of us wanted to live there, and so sold our portions of the land, most of it to our white neighbors, and a small portion to some of our former slaves, who paid for it in yearly installments of cotton until paid for. I lived with my brother John at the old home, until I was married to Lieutenant William Penn Lane, son of Rev. William K. Lane and wife Penelope Burford, who lived on their plantation near Goldsboro, their house later being burned by Sherman. My husband left the University of North Carolina and joined the 67th Regiment of North Carolina Calvary. Colonel John D. Whitford was colonel of the regiment. He was in service in Eastern North Carolina. In the Battle of Cobb's Hill, April 1865, near Kinston, he was one of seven men left of his Company: the others were killed or wounded. His picture, also my brothers' pictures, are in *Clark's History of North Carolina State Troops of the Confederacy*. These pictures were taken and left with their parents, when they marched away to fight for their liberty. This is true history.

An enterprising Yankee came south after the war and patented our homemade War Coffee, and called it *Postum*, and later on reduced the same to a powder and called it *Instant Postum* when requires no bag or boiling.

After passing through the horrors of war, we were subjected to the terrible time of the Reconstruction days and bayonet rule of General Denby, of the U.S.A. Government. At the first election after the war closed, the ignorant Negroes of the South were given the privilege of voting. There being so many more Negroes in the South than white men and they being instigated (by Yankees, who remained in the South) to all kinds of lawlessness, no one's life was safe, and a woman dared not leave her yard without a pistol for protection. This was when the order of the Klu Klux Klan was organized and every decent white man became a member. Oh! … The horrors of Reconstruction Days!

(Signed)
*Harriet Cobb Lane*

# Incidents of the Invasion of North Carolina

On the tenth of March, less than a month after the burning of Columbia, Kilpatrick's cavalry overran Fayetteville, North Carolina, and the surrounding country. At Manchester, these troopers came upon the estate of the aged Mr. Duncan Murchison. Here Miss Kate P. Goodridge and her sister were "refugeeing" from Norfolk. The Goodridge family was originally from New England; but, like practically all New England settlers in the South, they were heart and soul with the cause of the Confederacy, and they bore privations with a heroism no less than the native Southerners. Five of the Goodridge family had enlisted in the Confederate service.

As in the case of thousands of other private houses, the Murchison mansion was thoroughly ransacked; but many of the family valuables had been hidden so successfully that some of the soldiers became, enraged at not securing greater booty; in spite of protests, they burst into the room of a young girl who was in the last stages of typhoid fever. The child was taken from the bed in which she lay and died while the bed and the room were being searched for money and jewelry. An officer, whose name indicated foreign birth or extraction, was appealed to; but his answer to the Goodridge ladies was: "Go ahead, boys, do all the mischief you can."

Although more than seventy years old, Mr. Murchison, a kinsman of Sir Roderick Murchison, was threatened with death; but Miss Phoebe Goodridge fell on her knees and begged for his life. Consequently, the soldiers refrained from carrying out their threat, but dragged Mr. Murchison, half-clad, into the nearby swamps, where he was compelled to stay until the raiders had gone away. The troopers slashed the family portraits with their swords, broke up much of the furniture, and poured molasses into the piano. Everything in the nature of food was destroyed. Cattle and poultry were driven off or shot. All granaries of corn and wheat were torn open and the contents carried off or ruined. Consequently, the members of the family were, like many of the women of Georgia and South Carolina, compelled to live on scattered grains left by the cavalry horses, which they washed and made over into what they called "big hominy."

In this carnival of destruction, it should be noted that not one act of vandalism was recorded against the happy record of more than five hundred Negroes of this and adjoining estates, although they were given every incentive to rise up and pillage and possess the property of the helpless women. The Murchison plantation was twelve miles from the town of Fayetteville.

In connection with the story of this cavalry raid, it may be added that Mrs. Monroe, a woman of Scotch blood and a dependent of the Murchison family, was given a very valuable watch for safekeeping. In some manner, the raiders heard of it. They visited Mrs. Monroe and although they choked her into insensibility, they failed to get the watch. After the raid, the faithful woman returned the watch to Miss Goodridge, triumphantly exclaiming: "They nae got it! They nae got it!" When complimented on her bravery, she replied: "There is but one time to die and it might as well be now."

There is an interesting anecdote of a Miss Tillinghast of the town of Fayetteville. Miss Tillinghast, like the Goodridges, was of New England parentage. While her house was being ransacked, she stood on the steps and, with true Puritan fervor, read, for the benefit of her unwelcome visitors, the 109th Psalm, wherein the Psalmist commends the thought that the days of the unmerciful *"be few"* and that their names *"be blotted out."*

## Camouflage Against Raiders

The reminiscences of Mrs. Rachel Pearsall, while they cannot be here given in full, furnish an admirable illustration of the ingenuity of the women and the faithfulness of the greater number of the slaves, or, as they were usually called, servants.

Mrs. Pearsall lived on a farm near Kenansville, Dublin County, the site of one of the most important factories for the making of swords or sabres in the South. Mrs. Pearsall writes:

When our soldiers were off, we began to prepare to make a living. The old men managed most of the affairs, and in our part of the county we got along fairly well until the Yankees began to come up from the eastern part of the State and make raids on us. Then what a time we poor women had!

The first thing they did was to demand the keys of the jailer at Kenansville. They then liberated the prisoners and burned the sword factory; they surprised some soldiers in camp there and took prisoners. They then went from Kenansville to Warsaw, taking all the horses along the way, cutting the telegraph wire, and destroying everything possible.

* * * *

Of the close of the war, Mrs. Pearsall writes:

I remember that near the close of the war, we heard of Sherman being on his march. Fearing that he might come our way, we began preparing for it by hiding our valuables. Our first thought was for our silver and jewels. These we hid ourselves, not even our servants knew their hiding place — then we hid most of the meat.

I had two faithful old servants in whom I confided; I had, them get the largest box they could find and bury it in the garden. We picked out the choicest sides of meat and packed it full. The darkies said, "Missus, de sides will do us so much mo' good dan de hams and shoulders, fur dey will do ter cook de cabbage and greens fur er long time."

We nailed up the box, covered up the hole, and planted the garden over it. When the Yankees came, our vegetables were several inches high. They dug in the ground everywhere else in their wild hunt for valuables, but they never suspected the garden. Besides the "rescue" of the sides, I saved twenty-seven hams without any assistance. I hid them under the landing of the staircase leading to the garret. I had Mr. Pearsall's gun hidden in there too, but took it out later, wrapped it in a buggy, robe, and old "Uncle Robin," my most trusted servant, hid it in a hollow tree. We had a nice new set of double harness which I saved by carrying it in the night to the house of our faithful black mammy, Phyllis. We took up some planks of the floor, put it under, and nailed them back. I hid my watch, chain, and jewels in a tin box that was wrapped in cloth that I had dipped in wax. My silver knives, forks, and spoons, I put in a stone jar and tied the waxed cloth over the mouth, then dug a hole in the middle of a large hen house and buried it. I tried to pick out places to hide my things where I knew I could find them when it was all over.

All of our servants remained faithful except the cook. She declined to take any part in the hiding of our things, her excuse for not helping was fear of the Yankees. I was afraid she would prove disloyal. Sure enough, when the Yankees came, she demanded the smoke house key of me and gave them all the meat we had not hidden, then emptied the pantries.

I had just made up all our tallow into fourteen dozen candles. The men took them, but as they were carrying them out of the house, the nurse grabbed one out of the box. This was the only thing left to light my house except the pine from woods.

The raid lasted for three weeks, and the cook fed the Yankees on the best she could find at my house and cooked for them what they brought in from other homes in the neighborhood.

They pillaged the house from cellar to attic, opened every drawer, closet, and trunk, taking such things as suited them.

They treated my father-in-law worse than they did me, and took all the ladies' best clothes and what silver they could find. My aunt, who had been brought to my father-in-law's for protection, was sick in bed. The Yankees thought she was playing sick and that something was hidden in that bed. They snatched her off and threw her down on the floor so they could tumble the bed upside down. They found father's best suit which had been hidden there. All the beautiful quilts which had been made by the older members of the family and were highly prized were put on the old sore back mules and horses and carried off. They brought out father's nice carriage, filled it full of meat, made the servants dress chickens and turkeys, which they hung all around the carriage, then hitched two mules to it and drove away. They had taken the beautiful carriage horses off, on the previous day.

After the first lot of Yankees came, my cook informed me that she could not work for me any longer, that they had threatened to kill her if she continued to do so. I told her that I wouldn't have her cook for anything as I didn't want any harm to come to her.

There was a good, free Negro woman living on the place and I said to her, "Matilda, will you cook for me?"

"Dat I will, Miss Rachel, I'll be glad ter git sumpin' to cook."

This made the old cook furious with me, for she thought she would have the pleasure of seeing me cook. She made many threats on our lives, including Matilda, the new cook, who for protection had asked to sleep in my house.

After the Yankees quit coming, I felt we must be doing something toward making a crop. Part of the land had been prepared for planting before the Yankees had taken the horses off. One day I told Matilda that if I only knew how to do it, we would go out and plant the field of corn near the house. She said that she knew how and would be glad

to help me. So with the help of a white girl, Betsy, who lived with me, we planted the corn. Matilda dug the holes, I dropped the corn, and Betsy covered it with a hoe. "I thought that if I went to work, it would stimulate the Negro men to take up their duties again. The people of Kenansville hired Federal guards to protect their homes during the raid and after it was over some of them went out through the country to see how the people had fared. They had heard of the awful threats of a few of the Negroes.

One had heard of the threats of my old cook. He came to see her about it and she acknowledged she had said all he had heard, but that she didn't intend to burn up "Miss Rachel" and do the things she had threatened. I plead for her for I thought he intended to give her a good whipping, and I knew it would be worse for me after that. He told me to go into the house. I went, and tried to take her with me, but the guard ordered her to go behind the barn. Just then I heard one of my neighbors coming down the road and I ran out to the front gate and plead with him to interfere. While I was talking to him I heard a gun fire and he said, "It's too late, he has killed her." The guard sent to the field for the Negro men to come to the house and ordered them to bury her on the spot where she had been killed. When he had left,

39 —

they, obeying my instructions, made a coffin, dressed her in her best clothes, and gave her a decent burial.

He told me he wasn't going to leave me there at the mercy of the Negroes and asked me where I wanted to go. My father-in-law lived about a mile and a half away, so I decided to go there. He ordered the men to hitch up a horse to a buggy to take me. They told him the Yankees had taken all the horses and every vehicle. So he offered to take me on his fine saddle horse. I had old "Mammy Phyllis" to get together a few clothes for my two little children. When I was ready, my neighbor saw that I hesitated about getting on the guard's horse, so he said, "Mrs. Pearsall, my horse is gentle, you get on, and I'll lead him to your father's." I mounted the horse and took the baby in my lap. My little boy, David, expected to ride on the horse with me, but the guard said, "Come and ride with me, little man," to which David replied, "I'm afraid, you're a Yankee." The guard answering said, "I wouldn't harm you for anything. Come and I'll take you to your grandfather's." We went and stayed until things were settled. I left my home in the hands of my faithful servants and when I returned, I found everything all right.

I reasoned with the Negroes about going to work and told them if they would plant and work the crop, I'd pay them for their services. They then went to work without the aid of horses or mules.

One morning they informed me that they had heard that the Yankees had left some old mules and horses at a deserted camp near Faison, so I advised them to try to get some. They were lucky in finding a horse apiece and an old sore back mule for me. They were awful looking but improved with good treatment and made a fine crop.

The Negroes were working very well and were loyal to me when Mr. Pearsall came home in the early part of the summer of 1865. We were all so happy to have our loved ones back! Very few from our neighborhood were killed, but a good many were in prison at the surrender and these did not get home for sometime afterwards. Notwithstanding our poverty, after the crops were laid by, we had a big picnic, to which all the soldiers and their families were invited. In the fall, when harvest time came, Mr. Pearsall divided the crops with the faithful Negroes and gave each one some hogs, so they were able to start life for themselves.

# My Personal Experience of War

## By Mrs. Winnie Suggs

I was a mere school-girl when Schofield's Army came through this part of the country at the close of the war, but I was well-known and I had almost lived out of doors since my brothers went to the army. I attended to having the crop planted and gathered as long as the Negroes stayed with us. We had saved about three thousand pounds of meat beside lard and other things and when we heard that the Yankees were coming and I had the Negroes to help me hide it. Our smokehouse floor was of brick, and I had one of our men to remove the bricks and dig two large holes under the floor into which we lowered a barrel of lard and another of cured hams. Then we replaced the earth above the barrel, and the brick floor was relaid. Then we hid nearly all the meat that was left in more convenient places. An old man came by and told Mother that the Yankees would not steal her things if they found that she had made no attempt to hide them. Then Mother told me to put all the meat and lard back into the smoke-house, but I did not have as much faith in the old man's opinion as Mother had, and I only replaced a part of the meat. I had concealed some of it so well that I knew it could not be found and I made that which I returned spread out and look as undisturbed as possible, and I did not mention the reserve to Mother.

I hid the portfolio containing my brother's letters on top of a sill under the house. It had no value except as a keep-sake, but I felt that I did not want the Yankees to handle it. Otherwise our house looked as usual. All the Negroes had left us except one woman with a family of little children. We had sent the horses away off in the woods, hoping that they might escape, but the thieves followed the tracks and found them easily.

A group of Yankees rode up about breakfast time while we were preparing breakfast in the kitchen, and asked for food. Mother, thinking to divert them from plundering, began to cook them some ham, but when she saw another group coming up with her horses she dashed the ham out of doors and refused to give them breakfast. These rode away and in a few hours our yard was full of Yankee soldiers evidently bent on plunder. They demanded the smoke-house key, threatening to break open the door. I was afraid of them and politely handed them the key. They took all the meat and I saw one come in with all the meal we had in a sack. I told Mother that they had taken all and left us without bread. She began to cry and when the man with the meal sack set it down on the floor, one of the Yankees told me to take it and sit on it. I did so, and for a while I kept the meal. They came in squads all day, each squad leaving us poorer. I was afraid to leave Mother a moment. At last a group of four brutal-looking creatures came into the yard, partly drunk. A Negro baby, four years old, was toddling about the yard. A Yankee took it up in his arms calling it pet names, and asked where the white folks had hid things. The little Negro tried to tell by pointing and saying, "Dock."

Dock, my little brother, was in the yard, and in another enclosure was a place where all the meat on the farm was dressed. A kind of gallows on which the hogs were hung after they were killed had a rope and pulley to swing the hogs up. As I looked from the windows I saw those brutal Yankees hang my little brother, and calling Mother I flew from the house like a fury. I no longer knew what fear was. I seized the collar of the Yankee who was drawing the child up to the gallows and shook him until he released the rope. By that time Mother came, and helped me to unhang the boy, who was as white as a sheet and shaking with ague. Mother put him to bed and those Yankees left.

When the next group came I reported the brutal treatment of my little brother to an officer who said he would have the men punished if he could find them, which was a very safe promise. While the whole house was full of Yankees searching and looting everything my attention was called to something and I left the bag of meal on which I sat when they were present. When I turned back I saw one of them going away with the bag of meal. We had nothing at all of which we could make bread. 1 saw a Yankee come from under the house with my brother's portfolio and letters. I met him on the porch and told him that they belonged to my brother who had been killed in battle. He replied that he wished the "d ___ rebel" was there, he would like to kill him again. "But," he added; "you may take the rebel letters." "Yes," I replied, and I shall take the portfolio too, and I seized him by the collar with one hand, and took the portfolio with the other. I gave him a push and he went over, leaving the portfolio in my hand. His comrades laughed and seemed to enjoy his discomfiture. I believed from that time that it was bad policy to show fear of them.

Mother seemed to think that we had fared worse than anyone else. In the afternoon she took me over to our nearest neighbor's, Mrs. Mewborn, who was a widow with a large plantation. When we arrived the same Yankees were looting her plantation. I saw my bag of meal, and taking it into the house. I sat on it until Mother was ready to go home. I took it home with me. Mrs. Mewborn's brother, Mr. Ben Hardy, was very sick and we went every day to inquire of her how he was, and to offer what help we could give. We found Mrs. Mewborn greatly distressed one day because she was not allowed to go to see her brother. There were pickets on the road, and the Army was camping at Mr. Hardy's house. With the confidence of youth, I proposed to lead the way with another girl, while Mother and Mrs. Mewborn followed. I had learned by that time that a bold front was the best attitude toward Yankees. I slipped my arm around my companion's waist and we went down the road burning a tune as though it were the most natural thing on earth. We passed the pickets, who looked us over without a challenge. On arriving at the house, our mothers were invited into the sick man's room, but we were given a seat on the porch, where the young lady of the house introduced us to two officers who were reading there. After bowing distantly, I ignored these men altogether. I was boiling over with indignation at the treatment of our people and with the indiscretion of a child, I longed to express myself. Turning to my young neighbor I said, "Well Nan, how do you like all these blue jackets around you?" She replied that she thought they were nice and her voice took on quite a "Loyal" tone. I drew back from her, folding my ample home-spun skirts about me as if fearing contamination.

"Oh!" I said, "Keep away. Don't let any of your Yankee dust get on me!"

"Nan," I said, "What if a gray jacket came and saw you here claiming such friendliness with the Yankees, how do you think they would feel about it? For my part, I shall not pretend that I am glad to have them here. I shall not pretend that I do not hate everything they do, and I wish we could kill the last one of them. While I was speaking a soldier whom we had passed on the road came upon the porch. He was furious and roughly told me that if he had known I had such sentiments he never would have let me pass.

A gesture from the officer silenced the answer on his lips. There were a colonel and lieutenant on the porch. Lieutenant Sweet rose, took off his cap and bowing to me, said: "Lady, *Southern Lady*, I want to tell you how much I honor you for your patriotism. I know well that you cannot be as glad to see a blue coat as a gray one, and I admire you for showing how you feel about it."

Mrs. Mewborn came out and told the colonel that a chest of tools had been stolen from her smithy and she would like to recover them. He politely gave her permission to search for them and take them wherever she found them. Lieutenant Sweet offered to go with us, and remembering what I had said about "Yankee dust," he walked a little in advance of us. He was undoubtedly the best bred Yankee I ever saw. A few feet away Cousin Nancy found one of her sledge hammers. I offered to carry the hammer, saying laughingly that I might need it to kill a Yankee. At the corner of the fence was a huge U. S. flag, the handsomest one I ever saw. Lieutenant Sweet took the staff of it in his hand and said: "Ladies, let we wave the good old union flag over your heads once more." Impulsively I raised the sledge hammer in a threatening manner and said, "Never! I'll kill you if you attempt it!"

"Why," he said, "don't you love the Stars and Stripes?"

"Yes," I said, "the stars and stripes are not to blame, but the men that bear it and the cause it represents, and you'll never wave it over me." That flag stood in front of an encampment of 1,200 men and the young lieutenant and I were in full view. I was an impulsive earnest young girl and at the moment I was oblivious of the fact that I was among enemies. The army seemed to take in the situation, as he stood holding the flag and I with hammer raised defying him. A voice from the field said, "Kill Him!" And a cheer went up from the Yankee Army. It seemed to me that every man in the 1,200 cheered me. He dropped the flag and raised his cap. Mother hurriedly proposed to go home. As we started Lieutenant Sweet offered to let me ride his horse, Fanny, and he would send an orderly to bring her back. I told him if I rode a Yankee's horse I should certainly not send it back as they had taken all my horses.

Mother and Cousin Nancy politely took leave of the officers but I called back that if I met Lee's Army I would come back and take them all prisoners. Mother began to cry and reprove me, saying I must learn to hold my tongue. She was afraid they would come and burn her home. But next morning the army had moved their camp. When Mother cried because she thought we had nothing to eat but the sack of meal, I confessed that I knew where to find some things that I had not taken back to the smoke-house. Our home was bare of everything that could be easily taken away. We shared what was left with the one slave who had remained, and her five little ones. One day I was alone in the house. A Yankee and a Negro rode up on two beautiful horses. The Negro stopped at the gate, the white man dismounted and hitched his horse at the door. He had a rifle. "Ah!" He said, looking around, "the boys have done the work pretty well." He called to the Negro to come in and help him to burn what was left.

"No," I said, stepping on the porch. That Negro knows better than to come in. If he comes in I shall kill him. I saw that the Negro did not offer to come, but the white man began to move the chairs into the center of the room and called to our cook to bring fire. She refused but he kept moving things and calling for fire, in order to move a table he placed his gun by the door. I saw my advantage, and reached it just as he realized what I was doing. I did not have time to aim the gun but I raised it like a club and told him that I would use it if he came near me. The Negro on horseback rode off as soon as he saw me with the gun.

"Hold up your hands," I said to the Yankee, and his hands went up. Now I said, "Go get on your horse." He did so, but he begged me to let him have his gun. He said he would have to tell what had become of it. The rifle contained fifteen loads. I looked at the Yankee and told him that I would return the gun if he would take an oath. He agreed. "Raise your right hand," I said, "and repeat the oath after me: I Swear before Almighty God that I will go home and never fire another gun at a Southerner." He raised his hand and took that oath, and I handed him the loaded gun. Somehow I felt safe in doing so. He took off his cap and said: "You brave girl. No man could harm you after such a daring act, and I wish for you only what is good," and he rode away.

The Yankees had done what they could to destroy everything, but we had our land. There were no horses, but back in the woods we still had a few cattle and we had to do something to get bread to eat. There was no one left to do the work except our one faithful slave, my little brother, and I. We caught a young ox that had never been broken. Dock stood at his head and led him while our cook ploughed the furrows, and I followed and planted the corn. While we were engaged in this primitive style of farming a squad of Yankees passed on fine horses.

"Take out your horned horse," said one, "and I will hitch my horse to your plow. I see you are planting a crop ladies."

"Yes," I replied, "you have stolen all we have and we must plant something."

"What have you to eat now? Better go North where there is plenty."

"No thank you," I said, "We want none of your help and before I'd go North and live among Yankees I'd live on pine sap till my crop could grow."

The Army at that time was beginning to leave North Carolina, and the Carpet Baggers and Negroes had not begun their awful reign of terror. Some officers who were gentlemen, saw some shirts that Mother had made. They called on her and asked her if she would make them some to take home. Mother had only Confederate money, and she wanted to buy a horse. I was weaving a new homespun dress, checked with indigo blue and white. I cut the cloth from the loom and Mother made three shirts, for which the officers paid her nine dollars. She bought a horse for that, and it proved to be a very fine one.

# Courage Displayed in the Face of Overwhelming Odds

## *Complied by Lucy London Anderson*

General William A. Smith, Commander of the North Carolina Division United Confederate Veterans, gives this thrilling story of a heroine of Sherman's raid in Anson County.

"When the Federal army commanded by Gen. Sherman passed through the southern portion of Anson County, January and February 1865, occupying a week in passing; the L. D. Bennett home lay in his track. His soldiers set fire to the gin house and burned more than 200 bales of cotton, the corn crib and contents, the grainery with its wheat, oats and field peas; robbed the smoke house and destroyed every thing that would sustain life. The way to conquer the South was to conquer the women of the South — the sustainers of the army in the field — the only way to conquer the Southern women was to starve them and their children. In this they reckoned without their host as the Southern women were unconquerable.

> *"No annals of the world has ever told*
> *Of grander, more unselfish sacrifice,*
> *More loyal hearts in God's paradise."*
> *And sacred scribe has never vet unrolled*

They hooked up two magnificent beys to the finest carriage in Anson County and loaded it with hams from the smokehouse and drove away — it was never seen more. They drove off or wantonly shot every horse and mule, every cow and calf. Flock of sheep and goats did not escape. Killed the peafowls, the ducks, guineas and chickens. The only feathered thing that escaped was a gander. For three or four days during the passing of Sherman's army, he was without food or water. Afterward he came out of hiding. The Bennett family kept it as relic till it became so old that a breadcrust, when given was carried by him to the chicken trough and soaked — softened so he could eat it.

"They carried off the watches and jewelry and silverware, not leaving so much as a teaspoon. Broke into and ransacked the trunks, bureaus and closets. The piano, sofas, dining table, bureaus and other large furniture was cut up into fragments with an axe. They did not spare the old walnut and mahogany bedsteads. Opened the ticks and scattered the feathers over the floors of the chambers, with buckets brought molasses (sorghum) and mixed it with the feathers by thoroughly stirring.

\* \* \* \* \* \* \* \* \* \*

"The five sons of the Bennett family were all in the Confederate army. Mrs. Jane Bennett and two daughters, Mary and Charlotte, were the only occupants of the dwelling. When the Yankees came the mother and daughters retired into one room, locked the door and gave up the other portion of the house. After they had destroyed everything, (took what they desired and tore up the balance) wrought their fiendish will in both stories and attic, the vandals approached the door of the room where the mother and maiden daughters were. This they found locked and were preparing to break the door down. Then it was thrown open by the elder maiden with a repeating gun in her hand. Said she "I will kill the first man who enters." They looked at the repeating gun, then along its shining barrel, saw the scintillating beads of determination in the flashing eyes of the heroic girl, and steady hands of the resolute girl behind the gun, and dared not enter. Thus she saved her honor and protected her mother and sister."

"A man would not be brave enough to resist a horde of determined men bent on mischief, pillage and vandalism, but Miss Mary Bennett dared to and did defy them. Seeing an officer in their midst she asked him for a guard to be stationed at the door, which was done.

"The above story and incident is literally true as heard from the lips of Miss Bennett, for I married this HEROINE."

Captain Ashe tells us of how venerable Bishop Thomas Atkinson at his home at Wadesboro on March 3, 1865, was insulted by Sherman's soldiers. Bishop Atkinson said, "when the Yankees entered the town I requested my family to remain in their rooms. A soldier entering the door with many oaths demanded my watch which I refused to give up.

He then presented a pistol at me, and threatened to shoot me if I did not surrender it immediately. I still refused and the altercation became loud and my wife heard it and ran into the room and beseeched me to give it up which I then did. He then proceeded to rifle our trunks and drawers, took some of my clothes from these and my wife's jewelry."

\* \* \* \* \* \* \* \* \* \*

When Sherman's army was passing through Clinton, Sampson County, some of the soldiers attacked the home of Robert A. Moseley, commander of the Home Guard, who had been forced on account of illness to return home from active duty. It was during the night that the Yankee soldiers entered the home. They pulled open the trunks and drawers in search of valuables, then threw a large feather pillow on the infant Robert Moseley, Jr., who lay asleep on his mother's bed. Like an enraged tigress Mrs. Moseley sprang up in defence of her baby, exclaiming, "would you murder a helpless child?" With an oath the ruffian said "the D____ little rebel ought to be smothered." Just then a scream of "brother, brother," was heard and Robert Moseley rushed to the room occupied by his wife's eighteen-year-old sister which had been entered by the marauders. After plundering the bedroom and terrifying the young girl and her two little sisters, Anna and Ida, the soldiers left with curses and threats.

This incident was given me by Mrs. Moseley herself now a lovely and cultured old lady in her nineties. Her delicate soldier husband passed to the Beyond soon after Sherman's soldiers attacked his home, leaving her (who had been raised in wealth) to face the poverty of reconstruction days with five small children. How this young woman showed pluck and heroism in raising and educating these as splendid men and women is another story. But the spirit was characteristic of our Southern Women of the Sixties.

\* \* \* \* \* \* \* \* \* \*

As Mrs. Mary A. Corbett, of Ivanhoe, Sampson County, lay in bed with a two days old infant, Sherman's soldiers, trying to terrify her into disclosing her hidden valuables, started a fire beneath her bedroom window, the flames mounting high. In order to save her fatherless babes, she gave the information.

\* \* \* \* \* \* \* \* \* \*

A thrilling act of courage was exhibited by Mrs. Henry Finch, of Johnston County. In retaliation for Wheeler's Calvary cutting off part of Sherman's army train, the Yankee soldiers locked Mrs. Finch inside her home and set fire to the building. This intrepid woman raised the window, jumped to the ground, pointed a gun and threatened to shoot, saying she preferred to be shot by them than burned to death. The soldiers admired her courage allowed her to walk over to the adjoining plantation. The home of Mrs. Lucien Saunders in Johnston was also destroyed, and through it all Mrs. Saunders showed this same splendid spirit which characterized our Southern women.

\* \* \* \* \* \* \* \* \* \*

Mrs. Evelyn Smith Beckwith, while refugeeing from Craven County at Smithfield, Johnston County, had a terrible experience with Sherman's soldiers. With no one in the house but herself and four small children, Negro troops, commanded by white men, came upon them and demanded hidden silver. One of the officers threatened to hang Mrs. Beckwith and the children, and burnt her home, finally saying, "Madam, do you know we sometimes divest the Southern women of their clothes?" This indauntable woman replied that she was not afraid of him, and that if he dared deprive her of her clothes he would never get on his horse again.

And these ruffians departed overcome by her superb fearlessness.

\* \* \* \* \* \* \* \* \* \*

The same fearlessness was shown by Mrs. Murdock White, a young woman of Sampson County. When part of Sherman's army was engaged in their destructive visit to Sampson County they came upon her house. With a pistol placed at the head of Mrs. White they demanded the hidden valuables. This courageous woman said, "Shoot, I'll never tell you where they are." — Whereupon the ruffians departed from the house disgusted.

*Drawn by one of Sherman's soldiers, this illustrates many of the incidents we are recording, where homes were ruthlessly pillaged.*

* * * * * * * * * *

The experience of Mrs. Rachael Foy, the widow of Enoch Foy, who lived near New Bern, was very harrowing. Her only son, Franklin, was a scout in very hazardous service for the army, a reward being offered by the Federals for his capture. As Foy was scouting in the district around New Bern bringing in valuable information, the Yankees, thinking he would visit his mother and his small children, (who lived in that vicinity) came out from New Bern eight hundred strong. In their efforts to capture Foy, they surrounded Mrs. Rachael Foy's home, locking her and her grandchildren in a room, giving all her keys to the slaves, making them rulers over her household. They camped in her grove for three days, not allowing anything to be carried to her, though some of her faithful servants secretly slipped food and water.

Finally the soldiers marched off without capturing the Scout Foy. In the home of Mrs. Gillette they encountered Confederate soldiers, and a skirmish took place in the large grove of this home. Mrs. Gillette was very ill and not able to be moved to a place of safety. In the excitement she rolled off her bed, a bullet passing through the bed where she had been lying!

* * * * * * * * * *

Miss Nellie Worth (now Mrs. George French, of Wilmington) when Sherman's army were devastating Eastern Carolina, had a Yankee present a pistol at her head and threatened to kill her if she didn't tell where the valuables were hidden. This courageous young girl though completely in his power, defied and dared him to touch her, refusing to give the desired information. Finding his threats were useless, the disgusted "bummer" left swearing, as Miss Worth expressed it, "I was the d____st rebel he had ever seen," (which I considered quite a compliment).

* * * * * * * * * *

The story of how a young girl of twelve years cleverly outwitted a Yankee officer shows that even the children were on the alert to help their Southland.

The home of Mrs. Robert Roundtree, near Kinston, was invaded by the Federal soldiers and pillaged. The officer in charge made the young daughter, Rose, (a beautiful girl of twelve) sit at the piano and play for him. After this he forced her to accompany him on a drive, while the frantic mother, unprotected, could only plead for her child in vain. This girl, tho young in years, sensed her danger, and as she and her captor drove past a thick wood she exclaimed, "There's where my brother has his company of Confederate soldiers." Her ruse worked well, for the Yankee officer immediately wheeled, threw the girl from the vehicle and dashed madly down the road. After this it was observed that the Federals who had been hanging around the vicinity, all disappeared, evidently believing that our soldiers were secreted there.

This girl was afterwards Mrs. William Kennedy, of Kinston, an accomplished musician and beauty of the Sixties.

\* \* \* \* \* \* \* \* \* \*

The behavior of Sherman's army around Faison is but a repetition of the treatment of the people where ever they went.

In the home of Mrs. Rachel Pearsal of Duplin county, her aunt, aged and ill, was thrown from her bed on the floor, so that they could look for valuables they thought hidden there.

\* \* \* \* \* \* \* \* \* \*

A very thrilling escape from death by the Yankees was made by Doctor James H. Hicks, the father of Miss Georgia Hicks. Sherman's army was encamped near the home of Mrs. James H. Hicks. This courageous woman with a sorrowful heart saw her husband, that splendid physician, carried away in the night by the soldiers on the pretext of attending a sick man. Mrs. Hicks pled with him not to go but his one thought was to relieve suffering. He was carried far away and when he was brought by hours later, he had the appearance of a man that had almost seen death. These ruffians hung this fine old gentleman up by the neck twice, in their endeavor to secure information as to hidden valuables. They finally released their victim who refused to divulge his secrets. Doctor Hicks, never recovered from this terrible shock and his wife never mentioned it, for she was almost prostrated over his treatment by these ruffians. In the same house lived Miss Rachael McIver, "sister cousin" of Mrs. Hicks, who said always that she never knew why, but she was never afraid of the Yankee soldiers. One day when a man came down stairs with his arms full of silk dresses, she ordered him to put them down. He laughed loud, jumped on his horse and galloped away.

\* \* \* \* \* \* \* \* \* \*

The Yankee troopers came upon the home of Mrs. Duncan Murchison in Cumberland County and in spite of protests, burst in the room of a young girl, who was in the last stages of typhoid fever, the child was taken from the bed in which she lay and died while the bed and the room were being searched for money and jewelry. Although over seventy years old Mr. Murchison, in spite of the pleadings of the women of his family, was dragged half clad to the near-by swamps, where he was compelled to stay until the raiders had left. Every act of vandalism was committed on this plantation, but the Murchison women bore it all with heroic fortitude.

\* \* \* \* \* \* \* \* \* \*

Mrs. John McDaniel of Cumberland County not only had her home burned by these soldiers but her husband was carried out into the woods and hanged to a tree in order to make him give up secrets of his valuables. His death was prevented by some of his faithful servants and family, who rescued him from this terrible fate.

\* \* \* \* \* \* \* \* \* \*

The home of Mrs. Thomas McDaniel in this same community was also burned after the soldiers had taken it as their sleeping place for the night, this was certainly a very ungracious way of returning "hospitality" — Both of these homes were ransacked and the furniture and all valuables demolished or stolen. The Yankees as they set fire to this residence were heard to exclaim exultingly: "Well we've burnt up another home of a d___ rich old rebel."

\* \* \* \* \* \* \* \* \* \*

Mrs. Robert H. Cowan, of Wilmington, suffered a most thrilling experience while refugeeing near Laurinburg. Surrounded by Yankees, with two of her children at the point of death, she was subjected to every conceivable indignity. They pulled the rings from her fingers while holding her sick child and kicked the cradle of the other one with the brutal remark, "That one is dead already," while he rested his loaded gun against Mrs. Cowan's chair. The gang of marauders yelling and cursing slapped the face of the aged grandmother as he pulled the watch chain from her neck. Another ruffian threw his arm around a young daughter, saying he had just come out of the penitentiary, which they could well believe. With the sick babies, Mrs. Cowan, with her mother and young daughters (afterwards Mrs. Junius Davis, James I. Metts and Louis DeRosset) escaped during the night to an old hut, where they lay hid while the Negro regiments and greater part of Sherman's army passed.

# When the Two-Horse Buggy Came Down the Street

## *By Mrs. Andrew J. Howell*

"When the Two-horse Buggy Came Down the Street" is a true story, and the conversation between the girls and the Northern officers is copied almost verbatim from a rather crudely written letter which Anna sent to her oldest brother, who had not yet returned from the army.

She feared he might blame her for her part in this exciting adventure, and explained her side of it in minute detail. She, also, told him in very forcible language that a "scalawag" cousin who lived across the street from Headquarters house was at the bottom of the whole affair. This I have thought best to omit. This man lived until I was a large girl, and whenever I looked at him on the street, I expected to see horns and hoofs. He was never again really respected after he took his stand with the Union soldiers.

The children were out on the front piazza, sewing. They were sitting close to the front railing, because they felt obliged to see as far up the street as possible; and, their view in that direction was, unfortunately, limited by the gable end of the house which reached quite across the piazza and almost to the sidewalk.

If they had cared to turn their chairs the other way, they might have enjoyed the vista of magnificent elms shading the quiet street which led down to the square and to the Academy. It had been a favorite walk with them, and might become so again; but not on this pleasant morning in the early summer of 1865. For this little North Carolina town of Salem was under military control, and the headquarters of the trimly-uniformed Tenth Ohio regiment were just two blocks up the street!

The girls were sewing tucks in their new Jaconet skirt with he tiniest possible stitches, and were talking in low and guarded tones. "Livie, I'll never do it, if they kill me," said Anna, and even her long curls were trembling with indignation. "Oh, Anna," breathed Livie, "would you dare —" "Yes, I'd dare! But, hush. Here comes mother."

Anna's mother had come out to rest a moment and to inspect the sewing, which must be neatly done, as a new dress in that fatherless household was an event, a creation, which must last a long time. It was a home in which rigid economies must be practiced, and only their two refugee boarders, little Olivia and her mother, saved them financially.

"You are both learning to sew very nicely," said Mrs. Clewell. "Come in to dinner now, and then, if you will go up town and buy the buttons, Mrs. Bayard and I will work on your skirts while you are in school this afternoon."

Had she been observing the girls more closely, Mrs. Clewell might have wondered why her simple suggestion brought such a flush to their cheeks, and such a steely light to their eyes. As they delayed a moment to fold up their work, they looked steadily at each other.

"Oh, Anna," said Olivia.

"You'll see," was the answer.

They knew that it was useless to ask if they might change their school dresses; Sunday dresses were not to be worn on ordinary occasions. So the only touch of elegance which they could add to their costumes, without inconvenient comments from their elders, was supplied by their treasured beaded bags, in which they always carried their tiny vanity boxes.

Olivia's box was oval in shape, green in color, with a white top on which was a wreath surrounding this inscription:

"My dear, combine Thy heart with mine"

Anna's box was round and blue. On its top a white dove perched on a plump white heart, and under it was inscribed:

"A Token of Regard"

Inside the top of each little box was a mirror.

Slowly they started up the street towards the new town of Winston, whose court house and stores were but a few blocks beyond the limits of old Salem. They passed one elm-shaded house after another; and then, arm in arm, their feet almost refusing to move, their fascinated eyes fixed themselves upon the sight which they dreaded to see, and yet had determined to challenge.

Just before them stood a large house, its piazza, according to the custom of the town, even with the sidewalk; and, on the piazza, sitting, standing, lounging, were men in blue uniform, the Tenth Ohio regiment. But it was not upon the soldiers that the eyes of the two girls were fixed at this moment. It was upon something else. They saw, stretching across the sidewalk, one end fastened to Headquarters' piazza, the other to an elm tree on the edge of the street, gaily fluttering and brightly waving — not the Stars and Bars — but the emblem of their humiliation, the Stars and Stripes!

"Livie Bayard," said Anna, in a voice that strove vainly to be firm, "Brother can say all that he pleases. If he can lower himself to walk under that thing, I can not. I have said I will not, and I mean it."

"But, Anna, suppose they say something to us."

"Let them say! Hold up your head and do not see them."

So, with great dignity but with trembling knees, Anna and Olivia walked on, looking straight before them, reached the corner of Headquarters' house, stepped slowly off the sidewalk, walked in the dusty street until well past the obnoxious flag. Then, stepping on the sidewalk again, they went on, apparently quite unconscious of the buzz of talk from the soldiers that followed them.

"Oh," said Anna, as they neared the place on their way back home, "I feel so nervous. They look at us so hard. Is my hair smooth, and my bonnet right?"

"Yes," Livie assured her, with a few deft touches to her own prim costume. "Suppose we cross the street before we come to the Big Coffee Pot, and pretend that we meant to come that way."

With tremulous steps, for all of their brave words, they crossed the street and, out of the corners of their eyes, they saw on the piazza of the house an even larger group of soldiers than had watched them on their way up street, but no apparent notice was taken of them.

When they reached home they boasted a little of what they had done, and both mothers smiled over it, but added:

"Please, children, be careful of what you do while the soldiers are here. But, do you see the time? Hurry on to school, and here is your excuse for this morning. No, no, leave your bags at home. You do not need those vanity boxes at school. Good bye."

By three o'clock, the two women had donned afternoon dresses, had enjoyed together their "Vesper" of sugar cake and coffee, according to the pleasant old Salem custom, and were sitting on the piazza, sewing more tucks in the Jaconet skirts when, suddenly, two Federal officers walked up the steps.

The poor ladies were greatly agitated, and their efforts at self-control could hardly deceive their unwelcome visitors, who told them briefly and formally that they had orders to arrest the two girls for refusing to walk under the flag!

Mrs. Clewell's trembling hand clutched the chair behind which she was standing.

"Gentlemen," she said, "surely there is some mistake. The girls are so young, and do not understand. "Perhaps," she added with pathetic eagerness, "you have come to the wrong house; it is not our girls you mean —" but her voice trailed off into nothingness; she knew they had found the house they were seeking.

"No, madam," replied the spokesman. "Young Misses Clewell and Bayard are the ones wanted."

"The girls are at school," ventured Mrs. Bayard.

"Well, tell them when they return to come at once to the Provost Marshall's office in the court house. Orders from headquarters." Then, with military precision, they bowed, and the blue uniforms disappeared around the gable end of the house.

Poor mothers! With no man to help them except Mrs. Clewell's young son, Augustus, a boy in years, but a seasoned veteran of the Confederacy.

The officers were hardly out of sight when Augustus came up, whistling. But the careless tune changed to something like a groan when he heard his mother's story.

"I can only go and see Colonel Platt," he said. "Those foolish girls! Oh, mother! Can you not make Anna behave?"

"Son, they did not think. Oh, I pray God that there may be no trouble."

Then the mothers sat down to wait-just to wait, as they had done so many times during the past four years. This time the ordeal was short. The old Grandfather clock in the hall had just finished striking the next half hour when, with a feeling of overwhelming relief "that left them weak and faint, they heard Augustus' cheery whistle and his call, "All's right for this time, mother. Colonel Platt was polite to me, and seemed surprised at my story. He said he had issued no orders to have the girls arrested. I cannot understand that feature of it, but that is what he said. And he added, 'Tell the young ladies for me that, if they do not wish to walk under the flag, they can go on the other side of the street, or go another way.' So, mother, dear, see about a little supper for a hungry fellow, will you?"

But Augustus knew enough of martial rule to realize that such incidents might not always be taken so lightly; and he slipped quietly out and went down street to meet the girls as they strolled slowly home after school.

"Girls," he exclaimed angrily, pouring into their astonished ears the story of the afternoon; "Don't you know they can put you in jail if they want to? It can not humiliate you half as much as it does me to submit to that flag. I couldn't tell you if I would, what it has made me suffer. But it is here, and here to stay, it seems, and you must make the best of it. Do you hear me?" He added sternly, for he saw that, after the first expressions of dismay, the girls had exchanged one long, inscrutable look which might have meant anything.

Very little more was said of the incident at home, and it soon seemed forgotten.

About two weeks later, one Saturday morning, Mrs. Bayard sent the two girls up town on an errand. They crossed the street at their house, and re-crossed only after passing the Big Coffee Pot on the other side of headquarters.

On the way home they walked slowly. Perhaps to put off as long as possible the monotonous Saturday morning duties. And, also, it was barely possible that they wished to have a good view of the Bluecoats across the street. As they neared the place, it was all that they could do to maintain that appearance of haughty indifference which they considered the proper pose under the circumstances; for they saw that Headquarters' house was fairly alive with men, groups on the piazza, on the sidewalk, at the corner, all watching them.

Suddenly, as they were passing a house exactly across from Headquarters, an unaccountable impulse caused them to look up and, despite their brave front, they stopped, almost paralyzed. For there, stretching from the house to the street, and fluttering menacingly, was the duplicate of the Stars and Stripes across the way!

Not a word did they say. Their throats were dry and parched. Across the way, those who they thought were their foes. In front of them that which spelled to them deadly oppression. What should they do? With but a second's hesitation they turned slowly, and with a dignity beyond their childish years, they walked back the way they had come, followed by cheers and yells of admiration from their Northern audience.

"Mother," said Anna, when they had reached home by a devious route, "We had a very exciting adventure this morning." And both together, nervous and, uneasily triumphant, told the story.

"I hardly see how you could have done otherwise," said Mrs. Bayard slowly, "and yet, I wish it had not happened."

Mrs. Clewell said little, but, with a troubled face, she went back to her work in the garden, which was her care and pride, with its grass-bordered, exact squares of vegetables, and its trellis of grape vines on either side of the middle walk.

"Anna," called Olivia, after they had settled down to their usual tasks, "I am tired to death of cleaning lamps every morning."

"Not any worse than washing these dishes. I wish —"

"Let's just stop a moment and run over to the Belos, and tell the girls about this morning. Don't you wish we could have worn our new Jaconet skirts? You lock the front door, and we will be gone only a few minutes."

The exciting story was heard by the girls next door with absorbed and envious interest. For every girl in town knew the officers and their two-horse buggy, and most of them had a certain fearful and unholy longing to ride in that forbidden vehicle.

"Girls," exclaimed Anna, her black eyes widening with the thought, "suppose they should drive down street and stop over home."

The words were hardly uttered when, to their surprise and pleasureable terror, sure enough, the two-horse buggy of the Yankee officers came briskly down the street, and stopped with a flourish in front of Mrs. Clewell's door!

The two girls felt their knees go weak and their hearts were pounding madly. But, after a moment's peep in the mirror, and a little patting into place of their full skirts, they walked with as haughty an air as they could assume towards their house, where two officers were knocking impatiently on the closed door. One of them tried the knob and, finding it locked, walked toward the end of the piazza, calling sternly:

"I must have this door opened instantly, otherwise I will have it forced open!"

Before the girls could think of a suitably crushing reply, the door was opened by Mrs. Bayard, who had been finishing Olivia's neglected lamps. She bowed courteously to the unexpected visitors.

"We have called to see Miss Clewell and Miss Bayard," said the spokesman.

To be called "Miss" by these great military men! How Anna and Olivia did hope that the girls next door heard the dignified title!

"Come, girls," said Mrs. Bayard faintly. "Will you walk in, gentlemen?" she added, preceding them into the parlor which, in those days, was a cherished room, not to be used on ordinary occasions.

"Be seated, please," she said, as she opened the solid wooden shutters, and raised the windows with hands which trembled so violently that she could hardly adjust the wooden buttons which held them up.

There was one rocking chair in the room, which one of the visitors occupied, while the other seated himself on the long, cherrywood sofa. The girls, who had lingered outside long enough to see that the street in front was full of soldiers, and that one of them was holding a flag, now came slowly in and sat down on two of the green wooden chairs which were ranged primly around the room.

Meanwhile, the girls from next door had run into the garden to call Mrs. Clewell, who hurriedly joined the group in the parlor, quite regardless of the fact that her face was flushed from stooping, and that her skirt was stained by the morning dew. She, also, greeted the officers with all the courtesy she could muster, and then calmly seated herself by the man on the sofa, who turned a dull red as he heard a malicious little giggle from the children.

The spokesman broke the silence which ensued by saying:

"Ladies, I have some general orders here which I wish to read, also one from Colonel Platt." When he had finished, he turned to the girls and said, "What was your objection to passing under the flag?"

"Well," said Anna, whose face alternately paled and flushed, "as to passing under that flag, itself, I do not care, for I do not regard it any more than I would an old rag." And with keen delight she saw the veins in the man's forehead swell with impotent fury at her words. "It was because you tried to compel us that we refused. And, as to the other flag that was put out to intercept us, I would not have gone under that flag if my life had depended on it."

"Young lady," interrupted the officer who had not yet spoken, "I ordered that flag to be put up there."

"I am sure you should be very proud of it," she retorted scornfully.

"Anna, Anna," urged her mother faintly. But no one heeded her or Mrs. Bayard, who was imploring her daughter not to speak.

"Do you know," said the spokesman, "that even your greatest man, General Lee, did not refuse to walk under that flag?"

"Well," was the ready answer, if General Lee had refused to walk under your flag, you might have considered it insulted. But for two such insignificant persons as Livie and me to pass around it, I do not see how you could possibly care —" and her voice trailed off meekly into silence, so very meekly that Olivia laughed aloud, and even the officers seemed to have trouble with their facial muscles.

After a moment the spokesman continued:

"You will have to live under that flag, so you might as well walk under it."

"No, indeed," Olivia broke in; "we have both decided that we will never do that. We are going to live in either South America or Mexico just as soon as we are through school." And her youthful face was quite transformed with the heroism of her great resolution.

"Gentlemen," pleaded Mrs. Bayard, "you must remember that they are children yet. For four long years these thoughts and feelings have been growing in their minds, and it will take years to make them forget."

"Perhaps," said the officer darkly, "there may be a quicker way to accomplish that end." But he did not speak like a man very certain on that point.

At last the interview came to an end, and, turning to the girls, the officer said firmly:

"Young ladies, we are going to put the flag over your front door, and you" — looking at Anna — "will have to walk under it."

"Sir," she retorted, "there are two back doors and a dozen windows to our house, and I will climb out of the highest one before I will walk under your flag!"

As they were leaving, Mrs. Bayard said:

"May I know the names of the gentlemen with whose presence we have been honored during the past hour?"

"I am Major Stratton," said one. "And I am Adjutant Harkness'" said the other, as they walked out to give their orders regarding the flag to the waiting soldiers.

Within a few moments the two-horse buggy was gone, and the soldiers were all gone with the exception of one who was left to guard the flag which had been fastened across the front of the house, just over the front door. It was his uncomfortable duty, also, to see that the girls stayed indoors.

They stayed within quite cheerfully. Yes, why not? The outside world came to them; one group after another entering by the back gate, up the path between the grape vines, and through the back door into the house.

The parlor shutters were opened wide. The sun had one of his infrequent views of the carefully kept green-and-black store carpet. The wooden chairs knew their places no more. Behind the white muslin curtains sat the heroines of the hour, surrounded by admiring- and slightly envious-girls, who did not scruple to express very freely, indeed, their opinion of the flag, the colonel, and even the hapless sentinel without, whose red hair was the special subject of their caustic wit; until Augustus overheard them, and brought their elders to the poor man's rescue.

By and by came the early supper hour, and some of the girls remained to share the simple repast of fresh bread, country butter, cherry preserves and, of course, sugar-cake. For what Moravian family would be without sugar-cake for Saturday night supper?

"I wish I might offer the sentinel some. I think I shall." And Mrs. Clewell placed on the tray a piece of the sugar-cake and a cup of steaming coffee, carrying it as far as the front door. But she brought it back.

"The poor fellow seemed really grateful, but he said he dared not accept. You children have treated him shamefully. I am sure he would not be here if he could help himself."

The old town kept early hours. Very shortly Augustus went out to interview the sentinel. He found that Red Head had gone and another was on duty.

"May I lock the front door now for the night?" said Augustus politely. None but themselves ever knew how hard it was for these ardent young Confederates in the closing humiliations of the war.

"No," said the man, "orders are that the front door be left unlocked until further notice."

Augustus turned and walked slowly back. "Girls," he said sternly, "your fun may cost us all more than you know. Now they will not allow us to lock the front door. No, Mother, do not look so troubled. I am sure that none of us have any money to lose, and very little of anything else worth while," he added ruefully.

The next morning the church bell rang out sweetly, and soon the street was full of worshippers, carrying their hymn books, on their way down to the old Moravian church. One by one, as they passed the guarded house, they unconsciously slackened their pace, some of them smilingly glancing towards the front windows, whose muslin curtains would have a silent greeting in return.

It was a little harder today for the fun loving girls than it had been yesterday, for it was not the custom to visit casually on the Sabbath day, and they had little company. But they would have been martyred sooner than retreat from their high position. They studied their Sunday School lesson with half hearted zeal, they read their Sunday School library books, and, somehow, the day passed at last.

"Tomorrow," said Olivia, "let's plan to do a lot of things. Study for several days ahead, work on our samplers, and we can help your mother with that preserving she wants to do."

After dusk friends began to come in again. Augustus had placed a lantern half way down the garden walk, and one was burning on the back piazza. So that side of the house was quite cheery in contrast to the front, which the girls insisted on keeping perfectly dark. Several of the men of the neighborhood came in, also, to consult with the distressed mothers.

"Mrs. Clewell," they said, "we have thought of you all day, and, yet, it is very hard to decide how to help you. But tomorrow morning we are going up to see Colonel Platt. Perhaps we can come to some agreement."

"These children are not to blame, but" — hastily — "do not let them think too lightly of the affair, for they are liable to do something really serious if they are not held in."

"Oh," exclaimed Mrs. Clewell wearily, "Yesterday and today have been the longest days I have ever spent! I do not see how I can stand any more like them. Even the sentinel's tread is maddening to me. I thank you heartily for your kindness."

"Well, good-night, and take courage. We shall hope to do something tomorrow."

Gradually, one after another, the lamps in the town were blown out. Only in Headquarters' house did the lights burn late. The officers were asking themselves how they could manage to get out of a difficult situation without too great a loss of dignity. At last a silent footed messenger started down the street, and Headquarters' house, too, became dark.

Perhaps it was lack of exercise that made Anna restless that night. She slept badly. It was interesting to hear even a wagon rumble by. She welcomed the sound of the old nightwatchman's voice as he called out, now near, now further away:

"Twelve o'clock, and all's well!" "Two o'clock and all's well!"

She strained her ears to hear the sentinel's footfall. She dozed and waked again. Finally at the first hint of dawn, she dressed quietly and tiptoed towards Olivia's room.

Something in the hall stopped her. Something was different. What was it? Why, — yes-it was — the front door was closed!

Very quietly, indeed, she turned the knob, opened the door, inch by inch, peeped out

The people of the little town were early risers. Soon it was daylight and everybody was stirring. The first thing the neighbors did was to throw open their shutters and look over towards the house with the gable end to the sidewalk.

It looked just as it had done for many years. No sentry to be seen, no hated Stars and Stripes. The only sign of life over there was a girl whose black curls were fairly dancing with the vigor of her movements. She had a pail of water and a long handled brush, with which she was vigorously and thoroughly scrubbing that portion of the house which was just over the front door. And the neighbors caught these words of song ringing out cheerfully and happily:

*"Oh, yes, I am a Southern girl, And glory in the name —"*

# Bibliography

*Carolina and the Southern Cross,* Volume I, No. 9, November 1913.

*Confederate Veteran* magazine, Volume XXX, No. 5, May 1922.

*North Carolina Women of the Confederacy,* Lucy London Anderson, 1926

*Prize Essays Presented by the North Carolina Division, United Daughters of the Confederacy*, Mrs. S. L. Smith, Historian, 1933.

*Prize Essays Presented by the North Carolina Division, United Daughters of the Confederacy*, Mrs. S. L. Smith, Historian, 1934.

*Prize Essays Presented by the North Carolina Division, United Daughters of the Confederacy*, Mrs. J. J. Andoe, Historian, 1940-1941.

*Prize Essays Presented by the North Carolina Division, United Daughters of the Confederacy*, Mrs. Eugene Thomas Robeson, Historian, 1944-1945.

Letter by Mrs. Harriet Cobb Lane found in the attic of an old house near Bentonville, NC.

*Women of the South in War Times,* Compiled by Matthew Page Andrews 1920, The Norman Remington Co.

Richmond County, North Carolina Genealogy website www.ncgenweb.us

North Carolina War Between the States Sesquicentennial www.ncwbts150.com

# Other publications from

The Scuppernong Press

*Lincoln As The South Should Know Him*
................................................................... O.W. Blacknall

*Truth of the War Conspiracy of 1861*
...................................................................H. W. Johnstone

*A Story Behind Every Stone*
..................................................................Charles E. Purser

*As You May Never See Us Again*
............................................. Joel Craig and Sharlene Baker

*Additional Information and Amendments to the North Carolina Troops 1861 – 1865 Volume I & II*
...................................................................Charles E. Purser

*Memoir of Nathaniel Macon of North Carolina*
........................................................... Weldon N. Edwards

*General Robert E. Lee, The South's Peerless Soldier and Leader*
........................................................Captain Samuel A. Ashe

*A Confederate Catechism*
........................................................... Lyon Gardiner Tyler

More information available at www.scuppernongpress.com

The Scuppernong Press
PO Box 1724
Wake Forest, NC 27588

www.ingramcontent.com/pod-product-compliance
Lightning Source LLC
Chambersburg PA
CBHW071537080526
44588CB00011B/1704